1. Introduction

The Great Recession (GR) was the most dramatic economic downturn the US has experienced since the Great Depression of the 1930s. Tumbling stock and housing markets erased more than $15 trillion in national wealth in 2008, or nearly 10 per cent of real total national financial assets. As financial markets and the rest of the economy slowed to a halt, real Gross Domestic Product did not grow in 2008 and fell by 2.6 per cent in 2009, the largest decline in six decades. With the nation's economic growth abruptly halted, millions of workers lost their jobs. Between December of 2007 and 2009 total nonfarm employment fell by 5.7 percent – a loss of 8.3 million jobs – and the unemployment rate peaked at 10 percent.

The crisis brought about substantial economic policy response. In addition to the 'automatic stabilizers' built into Unemployment Insurance, SNAP, and the tax system, there were several major policy changes that pumped hundreds of billions of dollars into the economy in 2009 and 2010 (Burtless, 2009). The Troubled Asset Relief Program (TARP) helped stabilize the financial sector, using more the $400 billion to purchase or insure troubled assets, taking major stakes in General Motors, AIG, and Citigroup. The American Recovery and Reinvestment Act (ARRA) provided fiscal relief to state governments, reduced taxes, expanded TANF, SNAP, Unemployment Insurance and the Earned Income Tax Credit, and financed infrastructure projects, injecting more than $700 billion into the economy in 2009 and 2010. It is generally agreed that these policy changes, along with the monetary policy actions of the Federal Reserve Board, helped stabilize the economy and prevented the Great Recession from becoming a far worse economic event than it otherwise would have been (CBO, 2013).

The US economy halted its decline in the second half of 2009. Real Gross Domestic Product hit its nadir in the second quarter of 2009, and commenced growing in the second half. The seasonally adjusted unemployment rate peaked in October 2009 at 10 percent, and the lowest point in seasonally-adjusted nonfarm employment came in December 2009. Since entering the recovery period, which commenced in June 2009 according to the NBER business-cycle dating committee, the rate of growth has been slow, leaving millions of workers unemployed more than four years after the end of the recession was declared in summer 2009

The powerful economic shocks in 2008 and 2009, the policy response to the Great Recession, and the ensuing period of slow growth all impacted household incomes. This paper evaluates the combined distributional impacts of those changes. US Inequality had

risen in the decades leading up to the Great Recession, and this paper explores whether the recession or the expansion have interrupted or had any differential impact on those long-term trends (Thompson and Smeeding, 2013). It covers the impacts of the GR on household income inequality and poverty, primarily using data from the Current Population Survey (CPS). We also explore the degree to which the tax and transfer system mitigated these impacts in the GR, and analyze changes in the composition of income between earnings, capital, and transfers.

In the paper we show that changes in inequality and poverty during the Great Recession depend, to a great extent, on the population being considered and whether taxes and transfers are included in the definition of income. Using either market income or the Census Bureau's "Money Income," which includes some transfer income but does not net out taxes paid, inequality and poverty both rose substantially for all households combined. Between 2007 and 2009 the poverty rate among all people rose 15 percent under both the official definition, which uses Money Income, and market income. The distribution of household income also grew more unequal; the P90/P10 ratio rose 6 percent using Money Income" and 21 percent using equivalized market income, the Gini coefficient rose 1.1 percentage points using money income and 4 percentage points using equivalized market income. The distribution of workers' hourly wages also rose sharply, with the P90/P10 ratio and the Gini coefficient hitting record highs in 2009 and 2010.

Including taxes and a broader range of transfers than what is included in "Money Income" to create a measure of "Disposable Household Income" (DHI) suggests a different picture for poverty and inequality during the Great Recession. Between 2007 and 2009 transfer payments rose and taxes fell; the economic stimulus measures that helped halt the economy's decline in 2009 also softened the recession's distributional impacts. After adjusting for taxes, transfers, and household size, the Gini Index and the P90/P10 and P90/P50 ratios each declined modestly between 2007 and 2009. The increase in poverty was also blunted, rising only three percentage points (for individuals, using the experimental poverty thresholds and income measures recommended by the National Academy of Sciences (NAS)), compared to six percentage points using market income.

For the total population, taxes and transfers played an important role in offsetting increases in poverty and inequality that would have otherwise occurred during the Great Recession. The extent of that offset, however, varied across different group. In particular, policies appear to have been very successful at shielding and augmenting the incomes of the elderly, but not as successful for the working-age population. Between 2007 and 2009,

3

poverty rates rose 15 percent among working-age individuals, three percent among children, and fell five percent among the elderly. Instead of falling, as it did among the total population, income inequality was unchanged between 2007 and 2009 when measured among working-age households.

After 2009, however, as a slow-growing recovery took hold and the temporary economic stimulus measures began to phase out, inequality started growing again, regardless of the definition of income used or the age group considered. The P90/P10 ratio of equivalized DHI rose 4.5 percent for all households, and 8.8 percent for non-elderly households between 2009 and 2011; the Gini coefficient rose 3.0 and 3.7 percent, respectively.

Recent increases in inequality based on percentile ratios and Gini coefficients using CPS data are also largely consistent with the recovery of high-income and high-wage shares using administrative data sources. The long-term rise in the share of wages and incomes received by the top few percent of the distribution was halted temporarily during the great recession, but rose again in 2010 and 2011. The top one percent share of annual wages, based on analysis of Social Security Administration earnings records, dipped from 14 percent in 2007 to 12.1 percent in 2009, but had rebounded to 13.1 percent by 2011 (Mishel and Finio, 2013). The top one percent share of income, based on analysis of IRS tax return statistics, dipped from 21.5 percent in 2007 to 17.5 percent in 2009, but had rebounded to 18.8 percent by 2011 (Saez, 2013). Despite declines during the GR, top wage and income shares remain at historically very high levels, more than twice levels from thirty years earlier. The rapid recovery of corporate profits and the US stock market, both at all-time highs by mid-2013, suggest further improvements will follow for the top end of the income distribution.

At the other end of the distribution, poverty has remained at high levels since the official end of the Great Recession, particularly among the working-age. By 2011 the official poverty rate for households had risen to the same high rates seen in the economic downturns of the early 1980s and early 1990s. Among individuals between 25 and 64, after-tax and transfer poverty rates in 2011 were essentially unchanged from levels reached in 2009, while rates have declined among children and the elderly. A more comprehensive poverty measure – based on the US National Academy of Sciences recommendations – finds largely the same trend, though in-kind benefits and refundable tax credit helped mute the effect of the GR on poverty for some groups, especially families with children.

The next section describes the data and the methods used in the paper. Then we turn to discussing labor market conditions in the Great Recession and the period since. The fourth section of the paper discusses trends in income inequality, including data on top-incomes and the source-composition of household income. The fifth section discusses poverty trends, and the final section concludes.

2. Methods

Household income and poverty

In the analysis we use the Annual Social and Economic (ASEC) Supplement to the Current Population Survey (CPS). The ASEC, or 'March CPS' as it is conducted in March of each year, is a survey of approximately 65,000 households that has been conducted annually in the United States for more than 50 years. The ASEC asks respondents to provide detailed income, family, and demographic detail for the previous calendar year.

Our analysis uses data from the surveys conducted between 1980 and 2012, covering household income for the calendar years between 1979 and 2011. Our baseline figures use the Census Bureau's 'money income.' Money income is a broad income concept, and includes earnings, social insurance benefits, public assistance transfers, pensions and other retirement income, capital income, and other forms of income. Money income does not include capital gains income or reflect personal income taxes, social security taxes, union dues, or Medicare deductions. Money income also does not include noncash benefits, such as food stamps, employer subsidized health benefits, rent-free housing, and goods produced and consumed on the farm.[1]

In addition to calculating measures of inequality using money income, we also calculate measures of market income and disposable income. Market income removes public transfer payments from the census money income definition. Disposable household income starts with money income and nets out taxes, adding some transfer payments that are not included in money income. Taxes are estimated using the National Bureau of Economic Research TAXSIM model (Feenberg and Coutts 1993). Using the household income and demographic data from the March CPS, TAXSIM produces state and federal income taxes, including the Earned Income Tax Credit (EITC), as well as FICA social insurance taxes. We further supplement the baseline Census 'money income' definition by adding estimated food stamp benefits, now referred to as the Supplemental Nutrition Assistance Program (SNAP).

---

[1] Money income also does not reflect fact that noncash benefits are also received by some nonfarm residents which often take the form of the use of business transportation and facilities, full or partial payments by business for retirement programs, medical and educational expenses, etc. The definition is discussed in the "Income Definitions Appendix".

This estimate combines the CPS variables for food stamps receipt status, number of beneficiaries, and months of receipt with average monthly benefit amounts from the USDA. When considering long-term trends in any income measure, we include adjustments for top-coding in the March CPS, using the consistent cell mean series made available by Larrimore et al. (2008), and also account for the 1994 (Survey Year) series break by smoothing the relevant series at the break-point, similar to approach used by Atkinson, Piketty, and Saez (2011).

Both market and disposable income measures are divided by a standard equivalence scale to account for household economies of scale (the square root of household size.) We calculate several measures of inequality, including the Gini Index and ratios of key income per centiles, such as the P90/P50 and P90/P10 ratios, and also describe the composition of income (earnings, transfers, and capital income) and how those have changed in the GR. We calculate poverty rates, based on both the official poverty thresholds determined by the US Census Bureau, and also the relative measure of poverty (60 per cent of median household income) used by the European Union. We calculate measures of poverty and inequality for the overall population, and also for different age groups and educational attainment levels.

We explore the impact of changes to tax and transfer policies on poverty with the experimental poverty data published by the Census Bureau. We use the NAS-recommended poverty thresholds, which reflect regional cost-of-living differences, median consumer expenditures, and out-of-pocket medical expenses. We compare poverty rates by age group based on market income with those calculated using the expanded after-tax and transfer income also recommended by NAS.

Top incomes/wages

One important limitation of the March CPS is that it does not adequately capture income received by those at the very top of the distribution. The CPS income data are not only 'top-coded,' but the survey itself does not include sufficient numbers of high-income households to make reliable estimates of incomes at the very top of the distribution, the top one per cent or the top one-tenth of one per cent, for example. For a thorough discussion of top-coding in the CPS and how it impacts measuring inequality at the top of the distribution, see Burkhauser et al. (2008).

A number of other data sources can be used to assess inequality levels at the top of the distribution, including the CBO's 'comprehensive household income,' Internal Revenue

Service (IRS) income tax records and the Survey of Consumer Finances. We supplement the findings from our analysis of data from the March CPS by reporting some key findings from research that has analyzed inequality trends using these top-incomes data sources (Atkinson, Piketty, and Saez, 2011, Smeeding and Thompson, 2011). We also include discussion of related research focused on annual earnings, including papers by Kopczuk, Saez, and Song (2010) and Mishel and Finio (2013) using earnings records from the Social Security Administration. (Each of the income sources we use are more fully described in the Appendix on income definitions.)

Unemployment, labor force participation, and hourly wages

We use the Outgoing Rotation Group files of the Current Population Survey (CPS ORG), with data covering the period from 1979 to 2011, to examine how the Great Recession and other recent recessions have impacted unemployment, labor force participation, and hourly wages. As with income inequality, we calculate Gini coefficients and ratios of key wage percentiles.

3. The labor market during and following the Great Recession

The labor market fallout from the Great Recession proved to be both dramatic and persistent. With output shrinking throughout 2008, unemployment accelerated, with millions of workers losing their jobs. In the second half of 2009, however, the decline was halted. Real GDP hit its low-point in the second quarter 2009, and unemployment and employment followed suit, hitting highs (for unemployment) of 10 percent in October and lows (for nonfarm employment) in December (Figure 1). Growth in 2010 and 2011, however, was relatively slow, leaving millions of workers unemployed for long period despite the growth of GDP which surpassed the 2007 pre-recession peak in the third quarter of 2011 and which has continued to expand. By the third quarter of 2012, the unemployment rate remained more than 70 percent above 2007 levels, and nonfarm employment remained more than 20 percent lower.

<Figure 1 near here >

Rising unemployment and falling labor force participation among the working-age population

Among 18-64 year olds unemployment averaged 9.0 percent in 2009 and 9.3 percent in 2010. The overall rate of unemployment remained slightly lower than the 9.5 percent rate from 1983. Compared to that earlier downturn, long-term unemployment is considerably greater, and the rate of unemployment among most groups is actually higher than in the early 1980s. In 2010 the unemployment rates for all major educational-attainment and age groups hit 30-year highs. Among college graduates, the unemployment rate jumped from 2.4 per cent in 2006 to 5.6 per cent in 2010, and among those with advanced degrees it rose from 1.5 per cent to 3.5 per cent in the same period (Figure 2, Table A.1). But the largest increases – in absolute terms – were felt by younger workers with the lowest levels of education. Unemployment among workers with only a high school degree jumped from 5.3 per cent to 12.2 per cent between 2006 and 2010, and among those lacking a diploma it climbed from 8.6 per cent to 17.4 per cent. Highly educated workers continue to have lower unemployment rates, but the increases experienced since 2006 are proportionally as large as for less educated workers. All age groups also saw dramatic increases in their unemployment rates, with rates roughly doubling between 2007 and 2010. Workers aged 35–64 saw their unemployment rates go from around 3 per cent to nearly 8 per cent. The youngest workers (aged 18–24) saw their unemployment rate quickly shoot up from 9 per cent to 17 per cent, and the unemployment rate for somewhat more experienced workers (those aged 25–35) went from 4.3 per cent to 9.7 per cent.

All age and education groups saw unemployment decline in 2011, but rates remain at or above recent historic high levels for most groups.

<Figure 2 near here>

The official unemployment rate excludes 'discouraged' workers who have ceased looking for work. In 2011, 35 per cent of men aged 25–54 without a high school diploma were out of the labor force, compared with less than 10 per cent of those with a college degree (U.S. Bureau of Labor Statistics 2011). Labor force participation also declined for most age and education groups, although less dramatically than the rise in unemployment. The decline in labor force participation has been most prominent among younger and less educated workers. Participation fell by 0.7 per cent among college graduates and 0.2 per cent among those with advanced degrees, but it dropped by roughly 2 per cent for all workers with education below the BA-level (Table A2). For workers with less than a high school degree, the rate of labor force participation slid from 61.6 per cent in 2007 to just 59.4 per cent in 2010.

Most age groups also decreased their participation in the labor force. Among more experienced workers, including those aged 36–45 and 46–54, the declines were relatively minor, dipping by 0.4 per cent and 0.9 per cent, respectively, between 2006 and 2009. Among workers aged 18–24, however, the labor force drop off has been sizeable, falling nearly 4.5 per cent from 69.5 per cent in 2006 to 65 per cent in 2010. This recent labor force decline among young workers continues a trend present since the early 1990s. In each of the last three recessions, labor force participation has declined among young workers, and not recovered in the ensuing recovery, with the decline in the GR being the greatest. Between 1979 and 2009, the labor force participation rate of 18–24 year olds declined 10 per cent, while the share enrolled full-time in post-secondary education rose 10 per cent (Snyder and Dillow 2011). The opposite trend has held for older workers, who have steadily raised their participation rates since the late 1980s, through good and bad economic times. The participation rate in the 55–64 year old population climbed from 63.7 per cent to 65.1 per cent between 2006 and 2010, continuing a trend where participation rose in 21 of the last 24 years.

In sum, the picture is one of a state of continued labor market recession through 2011. Both Farber (2011) and Sum et al. (2011*b*, *c*) suggest that the numbers of displaced workers – those losing their jobs – and the numbers of long term unemployed were at an all-time high in 2010. Howell and Azizoglu (2011) show that new hires and job openings were at a decade long low in 2010, while permanent job losers were at an all-time high over this same period. The full effect of the GR on employment therefore is not known with certainty. Estimates from mid-2013 suggest that employment will not return to pre-recession employment levels until sometime between 2017 and 2020 (Looney and Greenstone, 2012, updated). And, there is a real concern that even rapid economic growth with low unemployment will fail to produce meaningful employment gains for some segments of the workforce. The main routes to the middle class for those with lower levels of educational attainment – manufacturing and construction – have narrowed and are essentially closed (Smeeding et al. 2011, Glaeser 2010). There has been considerable debate over whether the causes for continued high levels of unemployment in 2010 and 2011 were primarily cyclical or structural (Rothstein, 2012; Charles, Hurst, and Notowidigdo, 2013), but even a cyclical job loss that extends for 4-6 years becomes a secular issue almost by definition. Long term joblessness is very damaging to the career and life chances of all workers, especially younger workers and also negatively impacts family stability and the future of children in these households (Von Wachter 2010).

Falling wages and record high levels of wage inequality

In the face of a deep and sustained labor market downturn, real hourly wages can be expected to decline. Because so many workers have lost their jobs, however, the accompanying composition shifts in the employed workforce may potentially obscure falling wages. Trends in average real hourly wages, in fact, suggest modest growth in the downturn, but falling wages across the distribution in the early stages of a slow-growth recovery. Between 2007 and 2009, mean hourly wages rose from $20.59 to $21.04 (Table A2, panel A). These gains, however, were not shared across the distribution; wages fell at the 10th percentile (P10), rose modestly at the median (P50), but posted solid gains at the 90th percentile (P90). For these three points in the distribution, the change in real hourly wages between 2006-07 and 2009-10 was -1.9, 0.8, and 4.4 percent, respectively (Figure 3). Wages fell continuously for the lowest-paid earners since 2007, and in 2010 they were joined by the median worker, followed by workers at the 90th percentile in 2011. Between 2010 and 2011 inflation-adjusted hourly wages fell across the distribution. Falling wages at higher percentiles of the distribution during the recovery are consistent with composition shifts among the employed as low-paid workers found employment. Declining wages among more highly educated workers in their prime working-age years suggests that factors beyond the shifting composition of the employed may be at play in driving trends in wage inequality.

Table 1 illustrates the wage growth during the downturn and the recovery period for different age and education groups. Between 2007 and 2009, downward wage pressures were most evident among younger and less educated workers, while older and more highly educated workers continued to registered wage increases (Table 1, Table A2, panel C). Obtaining a bachelor's degree, however, did not make workers immune from wage pressures in the GR. Young workers (25–34 years old) with a BA saw their wages fall 0.1 per cent per year between 2007 and 2009 (Table 1). Older workers (55–64 years old) with a bachelor's degree experienced falling wages of an even greater magnitude. The only workers to experience notable gains during the downturn were prime-age workers with post-graduate degrees and training.

<Table 1 near here>

Since 2009 wage growth has turned negative for each age and education group. The biggest losses have been among the least educated, with two percent declines in real hourly in 2010 and 2011 for prime-age workers with only a high school degree, and the young, with 2.5 declines for 25 to 34 year olds with a college degree. Wages have fallen nearly as much, however, among the most-highly paid, with losses of 1.5 percent and higher for workers with advanced degrees.

<Figure 3 near here>

These divergent trends – wages rising at the top and falling at the bottom of the distribution – drove several measures of inequality to 30-year highs in 2010 (Figure 4). The graph indicates that over the 15 years preceding the GR, there were only relatively modest changes in these measures. (The impact of the series break, which is the result of a general redesign in the CPS, including a move to computer-assisted interviewing and expanded use of internal censoring for top-coded values, on measures of wage inequality in the CPS ORG is discussed by Mishel, Bernstein, and Schmitt 1998). The P90/P50 ratio fluctuated from year-to-year, but by 2006 remained at the same levels as in the late 1980s. After falling during most of the 1990s, the P90/P10 ratio exhibited modest increases starting in 2001, so that it had returned to 1994 levels by 2006. Starting in 2008, though, each of these inequality measures increased sharply. The P90/P10 ratio of real hourly wages, rose each year between 2007 and 2010, climbing from 4.4 to 4.8 (Table A2, panel B).

<Figure 4 near here>

Growth in each of these inequality measures halted in 2011. As the labor market shifted from a dramatic downturn to a slow-growing recovery between 2009 and 2011, the negative wage growth that previously was isolated at the bottom of the distribution became more widespread. Hourly wages fell for the median worker in 2010 and 2011, and they fell even at the 90th percentile in 2011.

4. Income impacts of the Great Recession

Because workers are typically part of a household unit that shares resources across several members, oftentimes including multiple earners, and because households are able to draw upon non-labor sources of income, it is important to go beyond wages or earnings and explore the impacts of the Great Recession on household income. Inflation-adjusted average household income (Census 'money income') fell each year between 2008 and 2010, but held steady in 2011 - the most recent year of data in the March CPS. (Inflation adjustments are made using the US CPI-U, and in all cases years are referred to according to the year in which the income was received, not the survey year.) In 2011 average real household income was 5 per cent lower than it had been in 2007, and remained at the lowest level in fourteen years (Figure 5, panel A). Median income for all households fell 7.8 per cent over the same period. While average money income fell for all households, and for non-elderly households, it actually rose somewhat for households headed by someone age 65 and older, reflecting a long term trend in elder incomes.

Income inequality measured using the money income definition rose steadily over this period. By 2011, the Gini index and the P90/P10 and P90/P50 ratios were all between three and seven percent higher than levels seen in 2007. (Table A3, panel A).

<Figure 5 near here>

Adjusting for taxes, transfers, and household size: Equivalized Disposable Household Income (EDHI)

In addition to the market factors driving employment losses and depressing wages, a host of actions by the public sector and individuals combined to influence household well-being during the GR and the following period. Automatic stabilizers (including Unemployment Insurance (UI), SNAP, and the Temporary Assistance to Needy Families program (TANF)) and discretionary fiscal policy all injected hundreds of billions of dollars into household incomes between 2008 and 2010. Total SNAP benefits rose from $37 billion in 2008 to $54 billion 2009, with 2.5 million new households getting 'food stamps'. Although it was only signed into law in February, 2009, the American Recovery and Reinvestment Act (ARRA) included hundreds of billions of dollars in tax cuts and increased benefits which did impact on household incomes during that year (CBO 2009).

The baseline Census 'money income' definition includes some sources of transfer income (UI, TANF, and Social Security), but it does not include others (such as the Earned Income Tax Credit (EITC) and SNAP, and it also excludes taxes. To reflect the influence of these transfers and taxes, we calculate a measure of net income which subtracts taxes (including federal and state income taxes and the employee share of social insurance FICA taxes) and additional transfer payments (including the EITC and SNAP benefits) from money income. To reflect household economies of scale, we then divide real net household income by the square root of the household size. The resulting measure, 'equivalised disposable household income' (EDHI), is a superior measure of household well-being, since an equivalent amount of gross money income results in a lower standard of living if family size is larger or applicable taxes are higher. This section contrasts changes in EDHI with the official income definition ('money income') and also with a measure of market income calculated by subtracting transfers from money income.

Accounting for taxes, transfers, and household size, average household income declined by only three-fifths as much – falling just 2.9 per cent between 2007 and 2011 (Figure 5, panel B). Non-elderly households follow the same trend, but elderly households saw their incomes rise over this period. The rise in inequality is also muted once these factors are included (Table A3, panel B). Instead of rising, the P90/P10 ratio is shown to decline modestly between 2007 and 2009 once taxes, transfers, and household size are incorporated into the measure (Figure 6, panel A). Figure 6 suggests, as Burkhauser and Larrimore (2011) have argued, that taxes and transfers have affected the income distribution differently in the GR than during previous recessions. In the 1980s, policy changes exacerbated inequality trends measured by the P90/P10 ratio for all households, but during the GR, taxes and transfers have reduced this measure of inequality. With the return to growth and the gradual phaseout of different portions of the economic stimulus policies in 2009 and 2010, though, the P90/P10 ratio appears to be rising once again.

<Figure 6 near here>

Trends in the P90/P50 ratio tell a very similar, if somewhat muted story. The increase in inequality evident in 'money income' between 2007 and 2009 is not present in the EDHI measure, but since 2009 the P90/P50 ratio for both series has risen at the same rate (Figure 6, panel B).

When we restrict the focus to include only non-elderly households, a somewhat modified pattern emerges for inequality measures. When all age groups are included, inequality in EDHI declines somewhat between 2007 and 2009, but when only non-elderly households are included, measures of inequality remain flat (Figure 7). Figure 7 is limited to the most recent decade, a period with consistent treatment of top-coded incomes.[2] The post-2009 surge in inequality is greater among the non-elderly. Incomes declined across the distribution between 2009 and 2011, but among the non-elderly the declines at the bottom of the distribution were larger and the declines at the top of the distribution were smaller. As a result, the 90/10 ratio of EDHI among non-elderly households increased nearly 9 percent,

---

[2] Top-coded observations are assigned the mean value, for each type of income, of the mean from all top-coded observations.

while the 90/50 ratio rose 3 percent, and the GINI index rose nearly 4 percent (Table A3, panel C). See also Smeeding et al. (2011).

<Figure 7 near here>

The impact of taxes and transfers, and the differential impacts between elderly and non-elderly households are even more evident when we compare trends between EDHI and market income. Table 2 shows that the Gini coefficient for market income rose 3.9 percent between 2007 and 2009 for all ages of households, but the DHI Gini fell by nearly one percent. The P90/P10 ratio rose nearly 21 percent using market income, but fell almost 3 percent in EDHI. The experience among the non-elderly, though, was different, such that the Gini coefficient for EDHI rose slightly between 2007 and 2009, and the P90/P10 ratio fell only a fraction of the decline seen by all ages of households. Also shown in Table 2 is the fact that the reduction in income inequality, expressed as the difference between market and EDHI inequality, for both the Gini coefficient and the P90/P10 ratio, is systematically greater among all households than for non-elderly households.

Since 2009 the increases in inequality, using market income and EDHI, are considerably larger among the non-elderly (Figure 8). It appears that the phase-out of the stimulus polices, alongside sustained high levels of unemployment, and a restoration of growth in the stock market and other sources of capital incomes are fueling a return to rising inequality seen in the decades leading up to the GR.

< table 2 near here>

< figure8 near here>

Shifting income composition

These comparisons of inequality trends indicated that households headed by the elderly and non–elderly have experienced different income paths though the Great Recession. Why did the elderly do better than the non-elderly? The elderly depend more on income transfers and investment income and less on the labor market than do the non-elderly. This basic fact of the 'by-sources' income distribution is well known and has been the subject of considerable discussion in recent years. The elderly who were already retired in 2008 lost some home value along with most other owners, but were generally invested in relatively safe portfolios, which protected their assets and income flows (Gustman, Steinmeier, and Tabatabai 2010). Older workers take up Social Security benefits at high rates once they pass age 62. The 46 per cent of elders who take up benefits between ages 52 and 65 are subject to an earnings test which discourages work in these age ranges (Smeeding et al. 2011). But those who wait until they reach their normal retirement age, 65 to 67 or more, not only receive higher benefits than at age 62, but are allowed to receive these social pensions without any penalty for earnings. Among the higher skilled elderly, employment has increased throughout the recession, owing in part to reluctance to retire and increased work after retirement. The success of the tax and transfer system in sustaining the incomes of, and mitigating inequality among, older households, and its failure to do so for non-elderly households is consistent with Ben-Shalom et al.'s (2011) assessment of US anti-poverty programs increasingly directed toward the elderly (and the disabled) and away from the young.

Analysis of the shifting sources of income, using the augmented income definition described above, confirms these prior analyses (Table 3). Table 3 contains a breakdown of the sources of income for the bottom, middle and top quintiles of elderly and non-elderly households, using the CPS ASEC. One of the well-known facts illustrated in these figures is that elderly households rely on transfer income for a much greater share of their income than non-elderly households. These transfers include public assistance and disability programs, but also, importantly, Social Security. Transfers make up 90 percent of income for the poorest fifth of seniors and nearly half of income for the middle fifth of seniors. For non-elderly households, transfers account for 60 percent of income in the bottom fifth and just 10 percent in the middle. Reliance on earnings is different, with the elderly getting very little of their income from earnings, and the non-elderly much more.

National Income accounts show that between 2007 and 2009 wages and salaries declined $151 billion, while transfers rose $422 billion (Table A4). Income from capital, excluding capital gains (and losses), declined $396 billion. High-income elderly households rely on capital income (including interest, rent, dividends, and retirement benefits) for roughly one third of their income, but capital income accounts for less than 10 percent of income in the top fifth of non-elderly households, although the CPS does not capture all sources of capital income. Combining the macroeconomic changes in income by source, with the age-related distribution of income by source, it is easy to see why inequality should increase more among the non-elderly. Among older households the affluent depend extraordinarily on capital income, while those with lower incomes are nearly entirely dependent on transfers. These two sources saw the most dramatic swings between 2007 and 2009.

The dramatic changes in labor market conditions, as well as government tax and transfer policies have resulted in substantial shifts in the sources of total household income. For most households, the earnings share of total gross household income ('money income' plus SNAP benefits and the refundable portions of federal and state EITC benefits) declined between 2007 and 2009 (Table 3, panel A). For the middle quintile group of all households and the bottom quintile group of non-elderly households, the drop was approximately six percentage points. In the top fifth, though (for both elderly and non-elderly households) the wage share of total income increased between 2007 and 2009, partially offsetting a declining capital income share experienced by both groups.

<Table3 near here>

The impact of public policy was relatively broad-based, with the transfer share of income rising and the tax share declining for nearly every quintile group (Table 3, panels B and D). The distribution of transfer income beneficiaries is very different for elderly and non-elderly households. (Transfer income here includes Social Security, Supplemental Security Income, Survivor's Benefits, Disability Payments, Public Assistance, Workers Compensation, Veteran Payments, Child Support, Alimony, Unemployment Compensation, SNAP benefits and the refundable portions of the federal and state EITC benefits and the child tax credit.) The transfer share of income rose 4.7 per cent for non-elderly households in the bottom quintile group and 3.4 per cent of those in the middle quintile group, but less than one per cent for those in the top quintile group. Among elderly households in the bottom quintile group, though, there was no change in the transfer share of income. The transfer share of elderly households in the middle fifth rose more than 6 per cent, but it also rose more than 3 per cent among elderly households in the top fifth.

The capital income share of household income also declined in the GR across most of the distribution, for elderly and non-elderly households (Table 3, panel C). Capital income in the Census Bureau's Money Income definition includes only interest, rental income, dividends, rent, trust, and retirement savings income. It does not include capital gains income. The decline in the capital income share was most notable for the top quintile group, where the capital share fell from 7.1 to 6.2 per cent for non-elderly households and from 38.3 to 32.6 per cent for elderly households.

Growth in top incomes/wages

Because of income top-coding and the presence of relatively few extremely high income households in the sample, it is not possible to use the March CPS to estimate inequality at the very top of the income distribution. In recent years a number of studies have demonstrated that much of the growth in inequality since the 1970s has been isolated to the top few percentiles of the distribution. To the extent that the top few percentiles are driving inequality, the P90/P10 ratios, and Gini indices calculated with the March CPS understate the level of inequality at any point in time and possibly the trend toward greater inequality over time. Because of differences in the income composition, it is possible that the Great Recession could have had a different effect on inequality at the very top of the distribution.

The data sources for top incomes experience an even longer lag-time than the standard household surveys, but we do have some preliminary evidence on the impact of the GR on inequality at the very top of the distribution during the GR and the period since. Analyzing tax data from the IRS, Saez (2010) finds that between 2007 and 2009 the income share of the top 1 per cent, including capital gains, dropped from 21.5 per cent to 17.5 per cent, and excluding capital gains income it dropped from 18.3 per cent to 16.7 per cent (Figure 9, Panel B). Since 2009, top shares have begun to rebound, with the top 1 percent share reaching 18.8 percent in 2011 (with cg) and 17.4 percent (without cg). The next-highest four percentiles of the income distribution (P95-P99) are the only other group with long-term increases in their share of income. Incomes in P95-P99 are not as cyclically volatile, though, and the income share of this group did not decline in the GR, rising slightly each year between 2007 and 2009.

Similar to other data on income and wages, these trends are in part influenced by composition shifts, as households with no taxable income drop from the data altogether, in addition to income changes for those who remain in the data. In their analysis of the tax data, Piketty and Saez (2010) assume that non-filing households have incomes equal to twenty percent of the average of incomes of filing households.

<Figure 9 near here>

Separate analysis of IRS data at the state-level confirms the rebound in top-shares in the wake of the Great Recession (for a discussion of the state level data, see Frank (2009) and Thompson and Leight (2012)). The overall trend in the state-level income share closely matches the more well-known analysis of the national level data by Piketty and Saez. The weighted average of states shows a 2.5 percent increase in the top 10 percent share between 2009 and 2011, compared to a 1.4 percent increase in Piketty and Saez (2013). The added value of the state-level data, however, is in the range of states. Figure 10 indicates that the top 10 percent share rose across the distribution of states. One state experienced a very small decline in the top 10 percent share (0.1%) between 2009 and 2011, and at the other extreme eight states saw increases of more than 3 percent.

<Figure 10 near here>

The decline and rebound in top shares is also present in wages. Using data from Social Security Administration earnings records, Kopczuk, Saez, and Song (2010) and Mishel and Finio (2013) calculate shares of annual earnings held by top wage groups.[3] Similar to the case for income, the top 1 percent share of wages fell in the GR (dropping from 14.1 percent in 2007 to 12.1 percent in 2009 (Figure 9, Panel A). The top one percent share had rebounded to 13.1 percent by 2011. Also similar to the case for top-incomes, the wage shares of earners in the P95-P99 rose slightly each year between 2007 and 2009.

The statistics calculated using the CPS showed rising inequality for market income during the Great Recession. This is consistent with the rising wage and income shares for the P90-P95 and P95-P99 groups, but misses the sharp declines in the wage and income shares of the top 1 percent between 2007 and 2009. The CPS-based figures are unable to capture what is going on at the very top distribution. The series based on IRS and SSA data, however, do not reflect the taxes and transfers that were previously shown to mitigate increases in inequality during the GR.

The "comprehensive income" series calculated by the Congressional Budget Office does include taxes and transfers, and also allows us to look at the top of the distribution, but is only available up through 2009 (CBO 2012). Comprehensive Income is much more expansive than Census Money Income, and by statistically matching the Census data to IRS tax return data, it includes much more in realized property income. Comprehensive income also includes imputations to reflect the market value of private and public health insurance.

Even with the base expanded to include the relatively equalizing influence of public and private health insurance, the CBO data show that the income share of the richest households has surged in recent decades (Figure 9, Panel C). The top 1% share of income

---

[3] Since self-employment income is not collected on the W-2 form, but instead is obtained from tax returns, where self-employment income is known to be under-reported (Toder, 2007), it is possible that these top shares are somewhat understated.

more than doubled between 1979 and 2007. Reflecting the highly cyclical nature of some of the capital income sources held by these high-income households, the top 1% share plunged dramatically in the early 2000s recession and in the Great Recession. Even in 2009, though, the top 1% share remained nearly 60 percent higher than levels from 30-years earlier.

The CBO income measure is broader than most income concepts, but it excludes large portion of capital income which accrues largely to the top of the distribution. Like the adjusted gross income used in the IRS statistics, comprehensive income includes interest, rent, and dividends, and realized capital gains (and losses), but the vast majority of capital income is not realized in a given year, including imputed rent on owner-occupied homes as well as accumulated financial and business wealth. Smeeding and Thompson (2011) use data from the Survey of Consumer Finances to calculate a 'more comprehensive income (MCI)' measure which combines standard income flows with imputed income to assets.[4] An update of Thompson and Smeeding (2011) to include the 2010 SCF data, shows that the top 1 percent share of income is between one and three percent larger, depending on the year, once estimates for unrealized capital gains are included. "MCI" rose from 17.6 percent in 1989 to 22.4 percent in 2007 (**Figure 11**). Between 2007 and 2010 the top 1 percent share fell back to 19.4 percent. IRS and CBO figures for comparable income groups (top 1 percent share of pre-tax income, including capital gains), show that the series derived from the SCF track the tax-based figures calculated by Piketty and Saez very closely. The SCF-based top shares are higher than what is seen in "comprehensive income," likely due to the equalizing impacts of health care benefits as well as the absence of substantial portions of unrealized capital income in the CBO figure, but the trends are similar.

Other recent research, by Armour, Burkhauser, and Larrimore (ABL) (2013), also imputes income to unrealized capital gains (losses) using a different methodology, but reaches the opposite conclusion, that incomes at the top of the distribution have fallen in recent decades. This research has been greeted with scepticism, in part because it relies on data (the CPS) not particularly well-designed to reflect asset ownership, the findings are quite sensitive to cyclical fluctuations in asset prices, and because of some of their assumptions lead to extreme and questionable results. (See Edall (2013) for a summary and review of some the critiques of the methodology used by ABL.) For example, a household with $100,000 in wage income and stock holdings whose value fell from $5.5 million to $5.4 million would have an income of zero using the approach of ABL, since they assign no value

---

[4] SCF income and MCI are both described in the Appendix.

to the stock of wealth itself. For this household, however, the remaining asset has considerable value, representing potential consumption and collateral, among others. The method of Smeeding and Thompson (2011), and that of Wolff and Zacharias (2006), recognizes the value of the asset stock and assigns it a return, which is diminished when the asset value falls, but does not become negative.

<Figure 11 near here>

Recent trends in top incomes – at least those observed by the CBO, in the tax data, and in "MCI" – are also consistent with analysis by Sum et al. (2011*a*). Sum et al show that in the early stages of the recovery – from mid-2009 to early 2011 – 88 per cent of the growth in US national incomes accrued to owners of capital (mainly business owners and corporations, but also pensions, rental property owners and stockholders) and less than 12 per cent to workers in the form of wages or benefits, with wage declines almost the same as employer benefit increases.

5. Poverty impacts of the Great Recession

As income declined, dramatically so for young and less educated households, poverty rose. According to the official U.S. Government definition of poverty (using the Census 'money income' definition), the share of households in poverty rose to 13.4 percent in 2009, and has continued to rise since, reaching 14.3 percent in 2011, reaching the same high levels hit in previous downturns (Table A3, panel D). We show poverty among household units for comparability to the grouping used in the income inequality section, but the Census Bureau prefers to present poverty figures for either individuals or families (families do not include single individuals or unrelated groups of people living together). Poverty among households had returned to the high levels from previous economic downturns in the early 1980s and early 1990s, while poverty measured among families remained somewhat below previous highs (**Figure 12**). The broader definition of poverty adopted by the European Union – set at 60 per cent of median household income – is considerably higher than the official US definition and fluctuates less over time. Over most of the last 30 years this poverty measure hovered at 30 per cent in good and bad economic times. Between 2007 and 2010, this measure of poverty rose from 30.2 per cent to 31 per cent, before falling back to 30.5 in 2011.

<Figure 12 near here>

The Great Recession's impact on overall poverty so far is comparable to previous recessions, coming close to, but no exceeding, levels last experienced in 1983. The impact across different demographic groups, however, is markedly different. Amongst younger households, including those headed by individuals under age 35, poverty rates hit 30-year highs in 2010 and 2011 (**Figure 13**). Between 2007 and 2010, the official poverty rate rose from 28.1 per cent to 37.3 per cent for households headed by individuals under age 25. For households with heads between 25 and 34, poverty rose from 14.3 per cent to 18.7 per cent in 2011. Indeed poverty rates ticked up for all types of units, except for those headed by a person 65 or over. Consistent with the other data reviewed above, poverty among elderly households fell during the GR, from 11.6 per cent in 2007 to 10.3 per cent in 2009, hitting a new 30-year low. In 2010 the poverty rate among the elderly rose back up to 10.6 percent, before falling back to 10.3 percent in 2011 (Table A3, panel D).

<Figure 13 near here>

Over the last decade, the rate of official poverty among households with children has been several percentage points higher than it is among households without children. This remained true during the GR (**Figure 14**). For those households with children, the poverty rate rose 3.8 points between 2007 and 2011, returning to previous high-points from the early 1980s and early 1990s. Among households without children, poverty rose by similar levels, but now exceeds high-points from those previous recessions by nearly 40 per cent, and 25 percent higher than the recession from the early 2000s.

<Figure 14 near here>

To understand the impact of changes in taxes and transfers on poverty during and after the Great Recession we turn to "experimental" poverty figures produced directly by the Census Bureau.[5] These "experimental" figures reflect improvements to the measurement of poverty recommended by the National Academy of Sciences (NAS) (Citro and Michael, 1995). The NAS recommendations, and subsequent Census Bureau refinements of it, alter the resources available to households beyond what is included in "Money Income" by adding other transfer income and subtracting taxes (similar in spirit to the DHI calculations used earlier in this paper for measuring inequality). The NAS measures go further still, however, by also adding in the value of subsidized housing and school lunches, and energy assistance, and subtracting work-related expenses including child care. Compared to the official poverty definitions, the NAS also adjusts poverty thresholds over time not by changes in the CPI, but by changes in median expenditures on necessities and adjusts for cost-of-living differences

---

[5] Figures accessed through CPS Table Creator (http://www.census.gov/cps/data/cpstablecreator.html), March 21, 2013.

across areas (using HUD fair market rents) as well as for out-of-pocket medical expenses. See Short (2011, 2012) for a more thorough explanation of these new measures.

We can use the Census figures to show the impacts of taxes and transfers, by comparing poverty rates using market income and the expanded version of income recommended by the NAS. Overall the experimental (NAS) measure results in a slightly higher poverty rate in most years; the 2011 poverty rate (for individuals) was 14.9 percent using the official definition and 16.9 percent using NAS-recommended income and thresholds. (**Table 4**). The most dramatic difference is in the age composition of poverty, though, by taking medical expenditures into account, the NAS measure results in higher poverty among older individuals and lower poverty among younger ones when compared to the official measures (**Figure 15**).

<Figure 15 near here>

Despite these differences between the official and the NAS measures, it remains the case that tax and transfer policies do a considerably better job of reducing poverty among older people than working-age ones. After accounting for taxes and transfers, poverty rose during the GR for the working age, and among some sub-groups it is has continued to rise since 2009. The post-tax and transfer poverty rate in the 45-64 age range was 10.1 percent in 2006, 13.1 percent in 2009, and 13.4 percent in 2011. By contrast, among the elderly, poverty either rose very little or actually fell, depending on whether we compare to rates from 2006 or 2007. Between 2006 and 2009, poverty among the elderly rose just 1.4 points, or 10 percent, using NAS definitions, far smaller increases than any other age groups.

Figure 16 contrasts poverty rates based on market income and the after-tax and transfer NAS income for different age groups, showing the trends relative to 2007. For all individuals, poverty rose 20 percent between 2007 and 2009 using market income, but "only" 9 percent using NAS income. Post tax and transfer poverty rose 15 percent for working-age sub groups, but fell 5 percent among the elderly. Since 2009, NAS-measured poverty has continued to decline sharply among the elderly, fallen slightly among those aged 25 to 44, and risen somewhat among those 45 to 64.

<Table 4 near hear>

<Figure 16 near here>

6. Conclusions and discussion

This paper shows that tax and transfer policies blunted much of the increase in poverty and some of the rise income inequality that we would have otherwise experienced during the Great Recession. These anti-poverty policies, however, were most effective for older households and for families with children. When we focus on non-elderly households, working-age individuals, and workers, we see record levels of hourly wage inequality, sharp increases in poverty and no change in income inequality during the Great Recession.

As the economy has returned to a slow-growing recovery and economic stimulus measures been phased out, inequality has begun to rise again, and poverty rates for working-age individuals remains at very high levels. Wage and income shares of the top one percent dipped in 2008 and 2009, and are now rising again. Broad-based inequality measures based on after-tax and transfer income are rising again, and poverty rates for 18 to 64 year olds remain between 25 and 30 percent higher than levels from 2007.

The elderly, owners of capital, and most high income households are doing well as we recover from the recession, and as capital markets have recovered faster than wages or jobs. Middle and lower-income households – those relying on earnings to provide essentially all of their income, those whose primary asset is their home, and those with something less than an advanced degree – are faring worse. The very steep decline in housing values (about 30 per cent from 2005 to early 2011) has led to higher rates of default and foreclosure and negatively affected aggregate consumption (Leonhardt 2011*a*).

The extended period of high unemployment that continues despite the recovery also threatens to have long-term consequences. Sustained high rates of poverty, especially among young jobless adults and families, is likely permanently scarring the futures of millions of unemployed younger unskilled adults. Without explicit steps to improve employment prospects for these particular workers, and to support the incomes of their children as we come out of the recession, poverty can be expected to remain high among this group.

References

Atkinson, Anthony, Thomas Piketty, and Emmanuel Saez, 2011. 'Top Incomes in the Long Run of History', *Journal of Economic Literature*, Vol. 49(1), 3-71.

Armour, Phillip, Richard Burkhauser, and Larrimore, 2013. "Levels and Trends in United States Income and Its Distribution: A Crosswalk from Market Income Towards a Comprehensive Haig-Simons Income Approach," NBER Working Paper #19110, June 2013.

Ben-Shalom, Yonatan, Robert Moffitt, and John Karl Scholz, 2011. 'An Assessment of the Effectiveness of Anti-Poverty Programs in the United States,' National Bureau of Economic Research, Working Paper No. 17042.

Burkhauser, Richard, Shauizhang Feng, Stephen P. Jenkins, and Jeff Larrimore, 2008. 'Estimating Trends in US Income Inequality Using the Current Population Survey: The Importance of Controlling for Censoring', National Bureau of Economic Research, Working Paper No. 14247. *Journal of Economic Inequality*, forthcoming.

Burkhauser, Richard, Shuaizhang Feng, and Stephen P. Jenkins, 2009. 'Using the P90/P10 Index to Measure U.S. Inequality Trends with Current Population Survey Data: A View from Inside the Census Bureau Vaults', *The Review of Income and Wealth*, 55(1), 166–185.

Burkhauser, Richard and Jeff Larrimore, 2011. 'Median Income and Income Inequality during Economic Declines: Why the First Two Years of the Great Recession (2007-2009) are Different', Unpublished paper, Cornell University, January, 2011.

Burtless,Gary. 2009. "The "Great Recession" and redistribution: Federal antipoverty policies", IRP Fast Focus #4, December; accessible at http://www.irp.wisc.edu/publications/fastfocus/pdfs/FF4-2009.pdf

Charles, Kerwin, Erik Hurst, and Matthew Notowidigdo, 2013. "Manufacturing Decline, Housing Booms, and Non-Employment," NBER Working Paper #18949, April 2013.

Citro, Constance and Robert Michael (Eds.), 1995. *Measuring Poverty: A New Approach*, Washington DC, National Academy Press, 1995.

Congressional Budget Office, 2009. 'Macro Effects of ARRA, Letter to Senator Charles Grassley,' March 2, 2009.

Congressional Budget Office, 2011. Economic and Budget Forecast: An Update, August 2011.

Congressional Budget Office, 2012. Average Federal Tax Rates and Income, by Income Category (1979–2009).

Congressional Budget Office, 2013. "Estimated Impact of the American Recovery and Reinvestment Act on Employment and Economic Output from October 2012 Through December 2012," February 2013

DeNavas-Walt, Carmen, Bernadette D. Proctor, and Jessica C. Smith, 2010. 'Income, Poverty, and Health Insurance Coverage in the United States, 2009.' Current Population Reports, P60-238. Washington D.C.: U.S. Census Bureau. http://www.census.gov/prod/2006pubs/p60-238.pdf

Edsall, Thomas, 2013. "What if We're Looking at Inequality the Wrong Way?" *The New York Times*, May 26, 2013.

Farber, Henry, 2010. 'Job Loss in the Great Recession: Historical Perspective from the Displaced Workers Survey, 1984-2010,' National Bureau of Economic Research (NBER), Working Paper No. w17040 May.

Feenberg, Daniel and Elisabeth Coutts, 1993. 'An Introduction to the TAXSIM Model', *Journal of Policy Analysis and Management*, 12 (1), 189–194.

Frank, Mark, 2009. "Inequality and Growth in the United States: Evidence from a new State-Level Panel of Income Inequality Measures," *Journal of Economic Inquiry*, Vol. 47, No. 1, 55-68.

Glaeser, E. 2010. 'Children Moving Back Home and the Construction Industry.' New York Times, February 16. http://economix.blogs.nytimes.com/2010/02/16/kids-moving-back-home-and-the-construction-industry/

Goldin, Claudia, and Larry Katz. 2008. *The Race between Education and Technology*. Cambridge, MA: Harvard University Press.

Gustman, Alan, Thomas Steinmeier, and Nahid Tabatabai. 2010. 'What the Stock Market Decline Means for the Financial Security and Retirement Choices of the Near-Retirement Population.' *Journal of Economic Perspectives* 24(1): 181–82.

Howell, David and Bert Azizoglu, 2011. 'Unemployment Benefits and Work Incentives: The US Labor Market in the Great Recession'. Unpublished paper, New School for Social Research, New York. *Oxford Review of Economic Policy*, in press.

Kopczuk, Wojciech, Emmanuel Saez, and Jae Song, 2010. "Earnings Inequality and Mobility in the United States: Evidence from Social Security Data since 1937," *The Quarterly Journal of Economics*, 125(1), 91-128.

Leonhardt, David. 2011. 'Men, Unemployment and Disability.' *New York Times*. April 8. http://economix.blogs.nytimes.com/2011/04/08/men-unemployment-and-disability /

Leonhardt, David. 2011a. 'We're Spent' *New York Times Review*. July 16. http://www.nytimes.com/interactive/2011/07/15/sunday-review/consumer-spending.html?ref=sunday-review

Looney, Adam and Michael Greenstone, 2012. "Understanding the "Jobs Gap" and What it Says About America's Evolving Workforce," Hamilton Project at Brookings Institution. http://www.hamiltonproject.org/papers/understanding_the_jobs_gap_and_what_it_says_about_americas_evolving_wo/

McLaughlin, Joseph, Mykhaylo Trubsky, and Andrew Sum, 2011. 'Underemployment Problems Experienced By Workers Dislocated From Their Jobs Between 2007 and 2009', Center for Labor Market Studies, Northeastern University. http://www.employmentpolicy.org/sites/www.employmentpolicy.org/files/field-content-file/pdf/Andrew%20M.%20Sum/Underemployment%20Paper.pdf

Mishel, Lawrence, Jared Bernstein, and John Schmitt, 1998. 'Wage Inequality in the 1990s: Measurement and Trends', Economic Policy Institute, December 1998.

Mishel, Lawrence, and Nicholas Finio, 2013. "Earnings of the Top 1.0 Percent Rebound Strongly in the Recovery," Economic Policy Institute Issue Brief #347, January 23, 2013.

Piketty, Thomas and Emmanuel Saez, 2007. 'Income Inequality in the United States, 1913-2002,' in Anthony Atkinson and Thomas Piketty, eds., *Top Incomes over the Twentieth Century: A Contrast Between European and English Speaking Counties*, Oxford: Oxford University Press, 141–225.

Rothstein, Jesse, 2012. "The Labor Market Four Years Into the Crisis: Assessing Structural Explanations" *Industrial and Labor Relations Review* 65(3), 467-500.

Saez, Emmanuel, 2010. 'Striking it Richer: The Evolution of Top Incomes in the United States', updated July 2010, Available at: http://elsa.berkeley.edu/~saez/saez-UStopincomes-2008.pdf

Sherman, Arloc, 2011. 'Despite Deep Recession and High Unemployment, Government Efforts – Including the Recovery Act – Prevented Poverty from Rising in 2009, New Census Data Show', Center on Budget and Policy Priorities, January 2011. http://www.cbpp.org/cms/index.cfm?fa=view&id=3361

Short, Kathleen, 2012. "The Supplemental Poverty Measure: Examining the Incidence and Depth of Poverty in the US Taking Accoutn of Taxes and Transfers in 2011," Census Bureau Discussion Paper, December 11, 2012.

Short, Kathleen, 2011. "The Research Supplemental Poverty Measure: 2011," Census Bureau, P60-244, November 2012.

Smeeding, Timothy and Jeffrey Thompson, 2011. 'Recent trends in Income Inequality: Labor, Wealth and More Complete Measures of Income', *Research in Labor Economics,* 32, 1–50.

Smeeding, Timothy, Irwin Garfinkel, and Ronald Mincy. 2011. 'Introduction to Young Disadvantaged Men: Fathers, Families, Poverty, and Policy', *Annals of the American Academy of Political and Social Science* 635, 6–23

Smeeding, Timothy, 2006. 'Poor People in Rich Nations: The United States in Comparative Perspective', *Journal of Economic Perspectives* 20(1): 69–90.

Snyder, T, and Dillow, S., 2011. *Digest of Education Statistics 2010* (NCES 2011-015). National Center for Education Statistics, Institute of Education Sciences, U.S. Department of Education. Washington, DC.

Sum, Andrew, Ishwar Khatiwada, Joseph McLaughlin, and Sheila Palma, 2011*a*. 'The 'Jobless and Wageless' Recovery from the Great Recession of 2007-2009: The Magnitude and Sources of Economic Growth Through 2011 I and Their Impacts on Workers, Profits, and Stock Values', Northeastern University Center for Labor Market Studies, May.

Sum, Andrew,Mykhaylo Trubskyy, and Sheila Palma. 2011*b*, The Unemployment Experiences of Workers in the U.S. Who Were Displaced from Their Jobs During the Great Dislocation of 2007-2009',Center for Labor Market Studies, Northeastern UniversityBoston, Massachusetts, June. http://www.employmentpolicy.org/sites/www.employmentpolicy.org/files/field-content-file/pdf/Andrew%20M.%20Sum/June%202011%20Unemployment%20Dislocated%20Worker%20Paper.pdf

Sum, Andrew, Ishwar Khatiwada, Joseph McLaughlin, and Sheila Palma. 2011*c*. 'No Country for Young Men', in Smeeding, Timothy, Irwin Garfinkel, and Ronald Mincy, eds, *Young Disadvantaged Men: Fathers, Families, Poverty, and Policy*, Annals of the American Academy of Political and Social Science, 635: 24–55.

Thompson, Jeffrey and Elias Leight, 2012. "Do Rising Top Income Shares Affect the Incomes or Earnings of Low and Middle-Income Families?," *BE Journal of Economic Analysis & Policy*, Vol. 12, No. 1, Article 49.

Thompson, Jeffrey, and Timothy Smeeding, 2013. "US Country Case Study," in Jenkins, Stephen, Andrea Brandolini, John Micklewright and Brian Nolan eds., *The Great Recession and the Distribution of Household Income.* New York: Oxford University Press.

Toder, Eric, 2007. "What is the Tax Gap?" *Tax Notes*, October 22, 2007.

U.S. Department of Labor. 2010*a*. 'Characteristics of the Insured Unemployed.' Washington, D.C.: U.S. Department of Labor. December. http://workforcesecurity.doleta.gov/unemploy/chariu.asp

U.S. Department of Labor. 2010*b*. 'Issues in Labor Statistics: Sizing up the 2007-2009: Sizing up the 2007-2009 Recession with Earlier Downturns Recession' Summary 10-11, December. http://www.bls.gov/opub/ils/pdf/opbils88.pdf

U.S. Department of Labor. 2011. BLS Statistics of Unemployment and Employment. http://www.bls.gov/bls/unemployment.htm

Von Wachter, Till. 2010. 'Avoiding a Lost Generation: How to Minimize the Impact of the Great Recession on Young Workers', Testimony before the Joint Economic Committee of the U.S. Congress. May 26. http://jec.senate.gov/public/?a=Files.Serve&File_id=c868a8d3-3837-4585-9074-48181c5320e6

Wolff, Edward and Ajit Zacharias, 2006. "Household Wealth and the Measurement of Economic Well-being in the United States," Annandale-on-Hudson, NY: Levy Economics Institute, Bard College.

Figure 1. Key Economic Measures of the Great Recession
Indexed Real GDP, SA Nonfarm Employment, and SA Unemployment (2007q3=100)
Shading Indicates trough of each series in 2009.

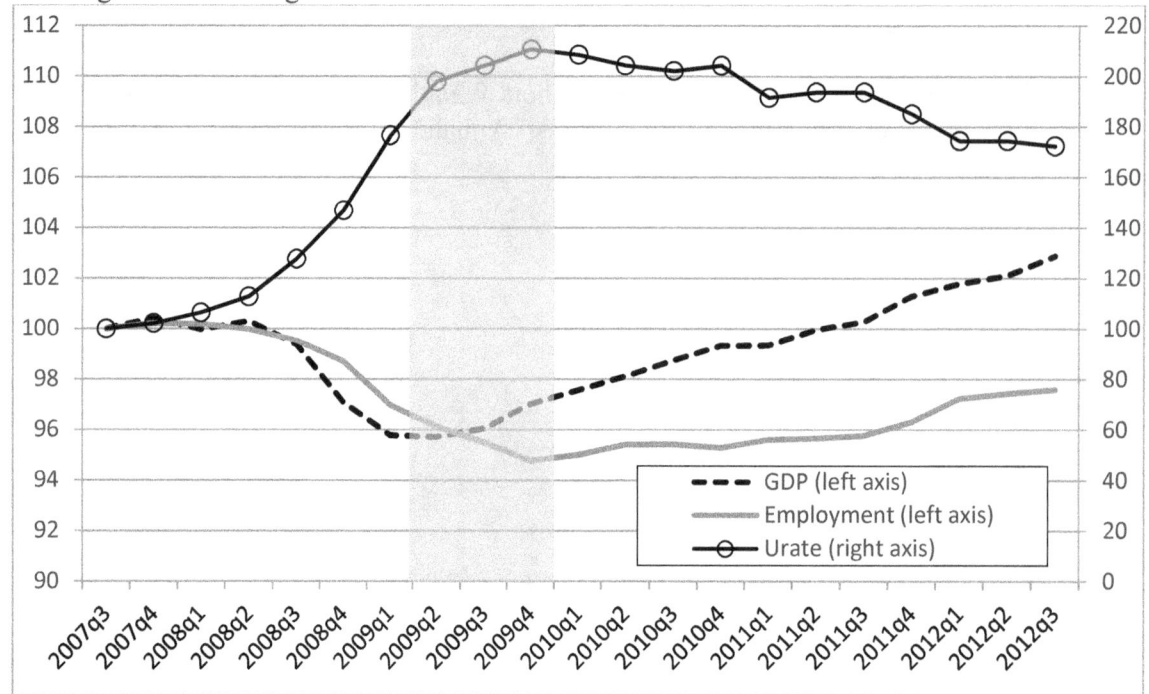

Source: Authors' analysis of BEA and BLS data.

Figure 2. Unemployment rate (%), by educational attainment, 1979–2011

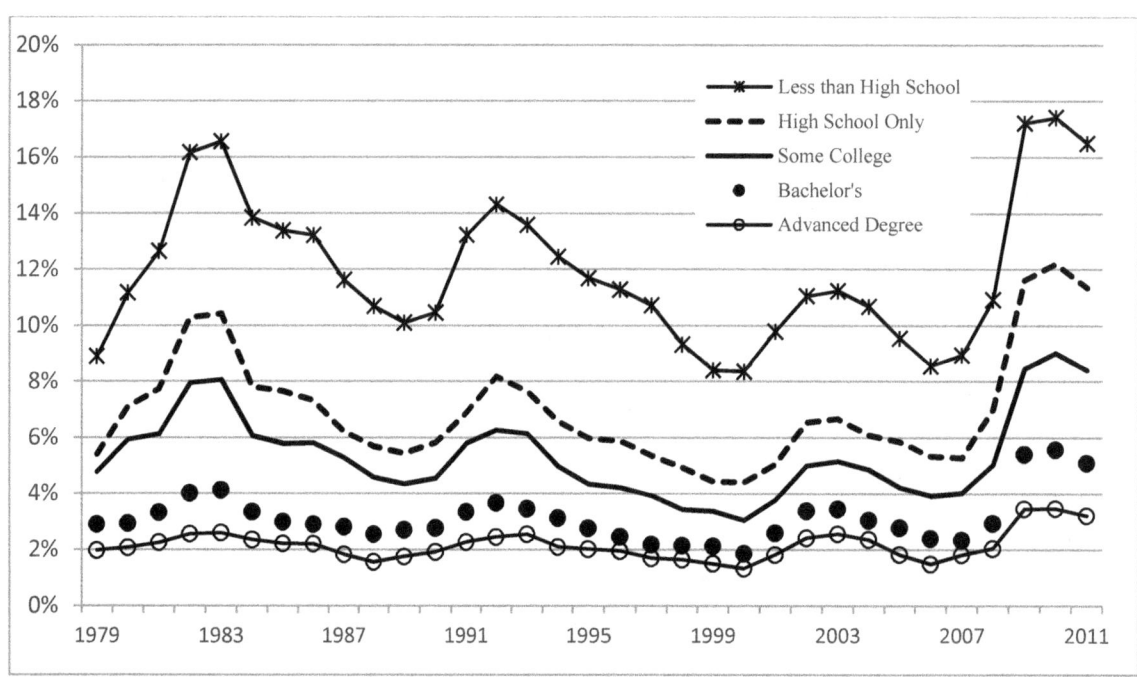

Source. Authors' analysis of CPS ORG Files (various years), CEPR extracts.

Figure 3. Trends in Inflation-adjusted (2011$) Hourly Wages, 1979–2011 (indexed 1979 = 100)

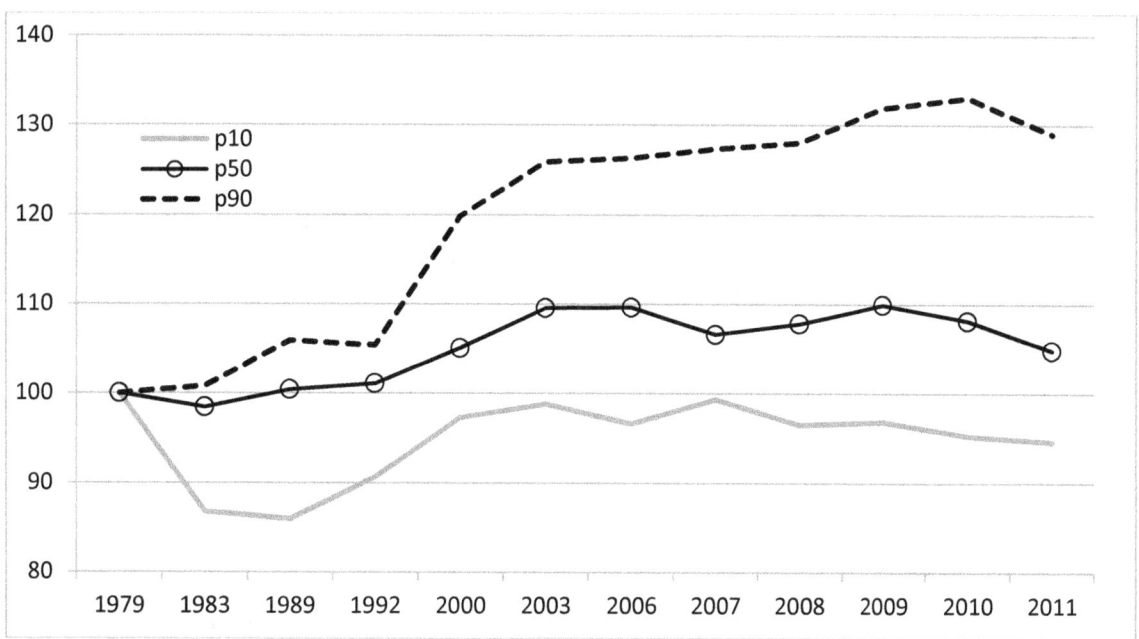

Source: Authors' analysis of CPS ORG Files (various years), CEPR extracts.

Figure 4. Hourly wage inequality, percentile ratios and Gini, 1979–2011 (indexed 1979 = 100)

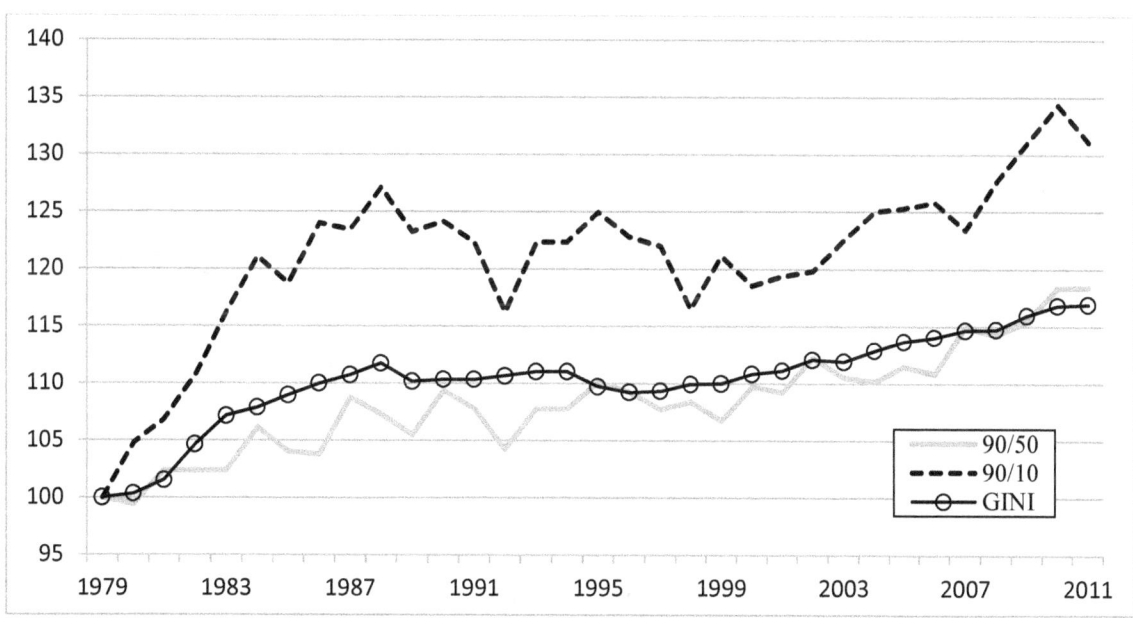

Source: Authors' analysis of CPS ORG Files (various years), CEPR extracts.

Notes. Estimates adjusted to smooth over the effects of the 1993 change in CPS data collection methods.

Figure 5. Mean inflation-adjusted household income, by age and income definition, 1979–2011

A. Census 'money income'

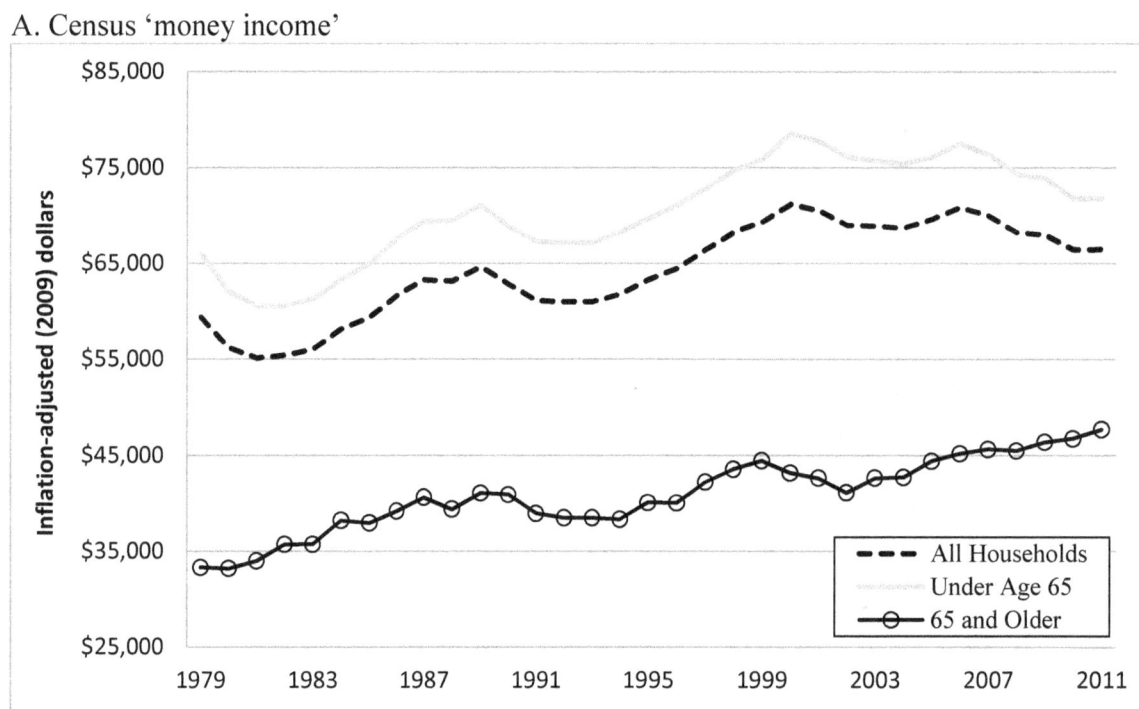

B. Equivalised disposable household income

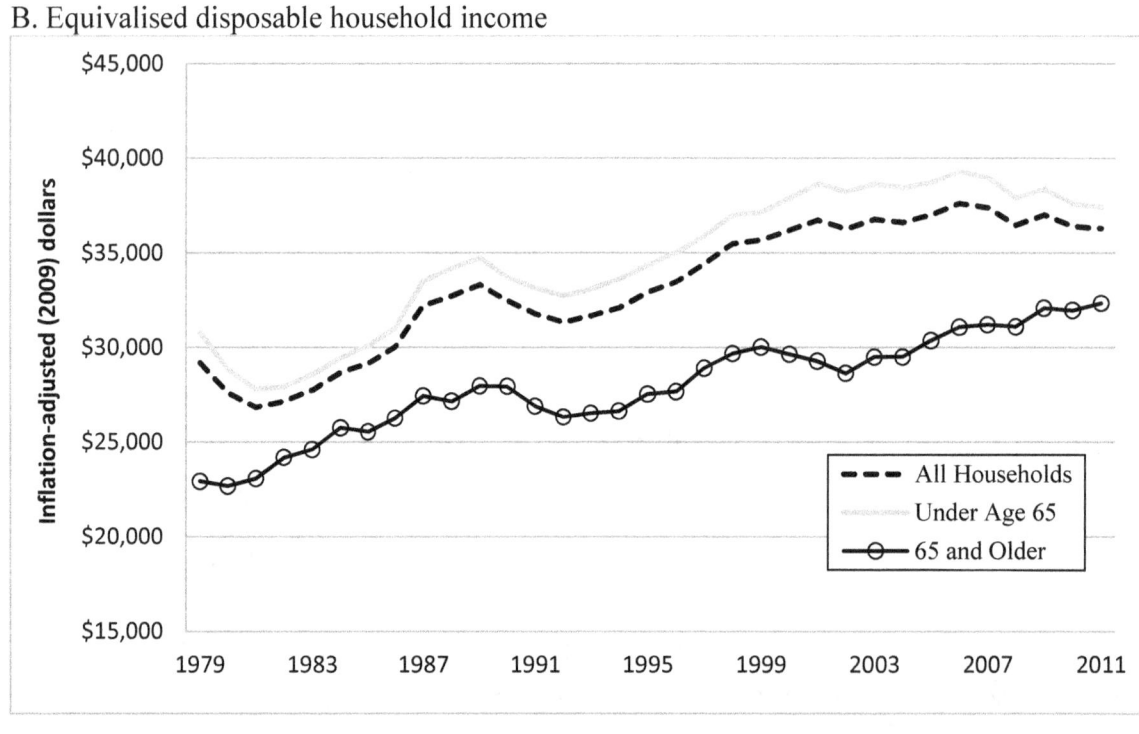

Note. Top-coded income values adjusted using consistent cell means (Larrimore et al. 2008), and series adjusted to smooth over the effects of the 1993 change in CPS data collection methods. Source. Authors' analysis of March CPS (various years), CEPR extracts. Adjusted for inflation using US CPI-U.

Figure 6. Selected household income inequality indices, Census 'money income' and equivalised disposable household income 1979–2011 (indexed 1979=100)

A. P90/P10

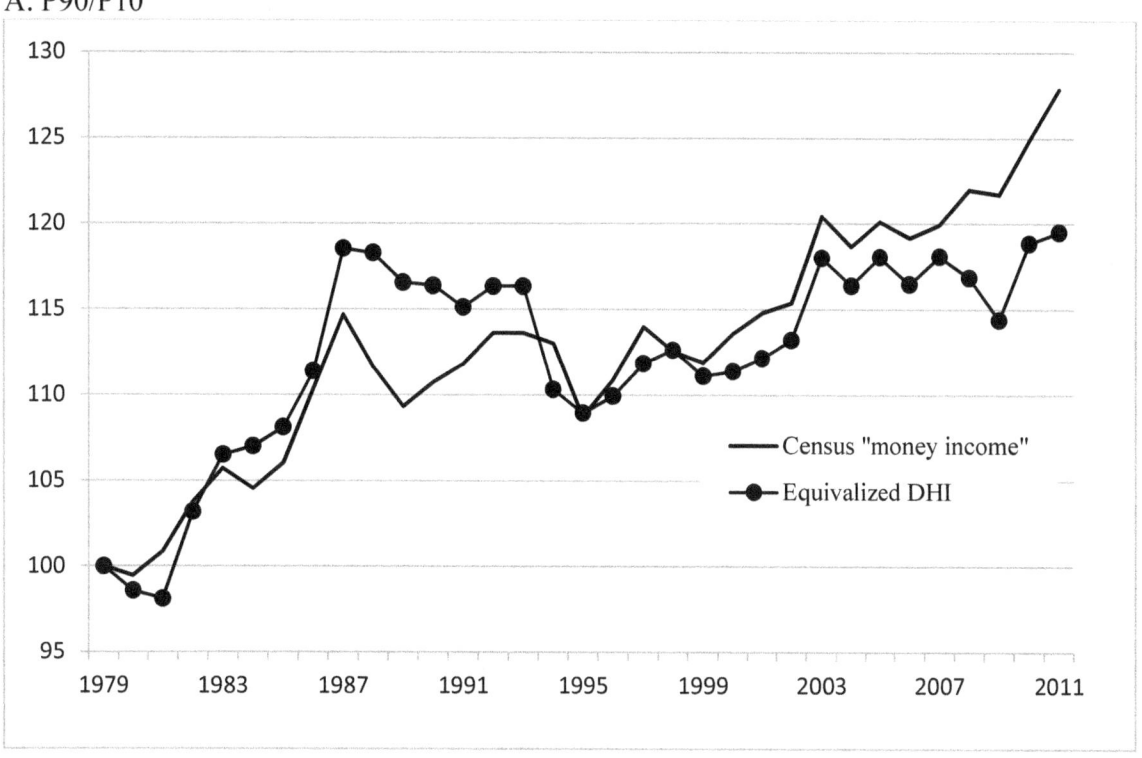

B. P90/P50

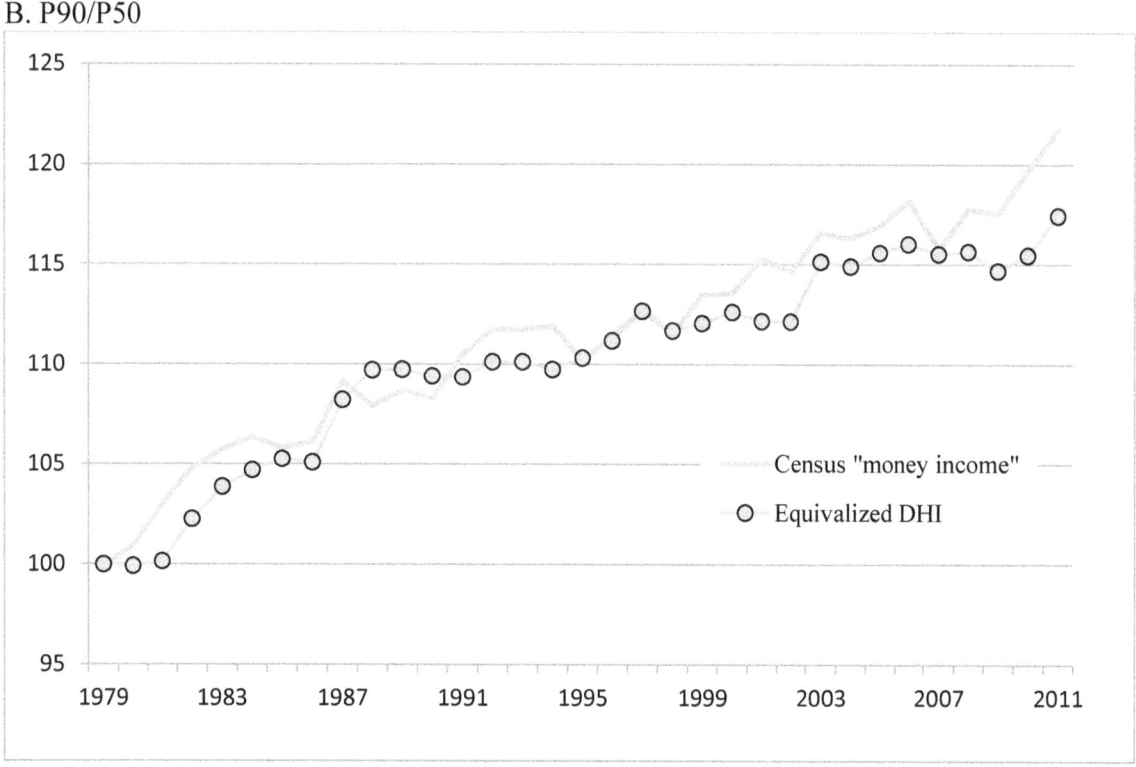

Note. Top-coded income values adjusted using consistent cell means (Larrimore et al. 2008), and series adjusted to smooth over the effects of the 1993 change in CPS data collection methods.
Source. Authors' analysis of March CPS (various years), CEPR extracts, and NBER Taxsim.

Figure 7. Inequality of equivalised disposable household income, non-elderly and all households, 2000–2011 (indexed 2000 = 100)

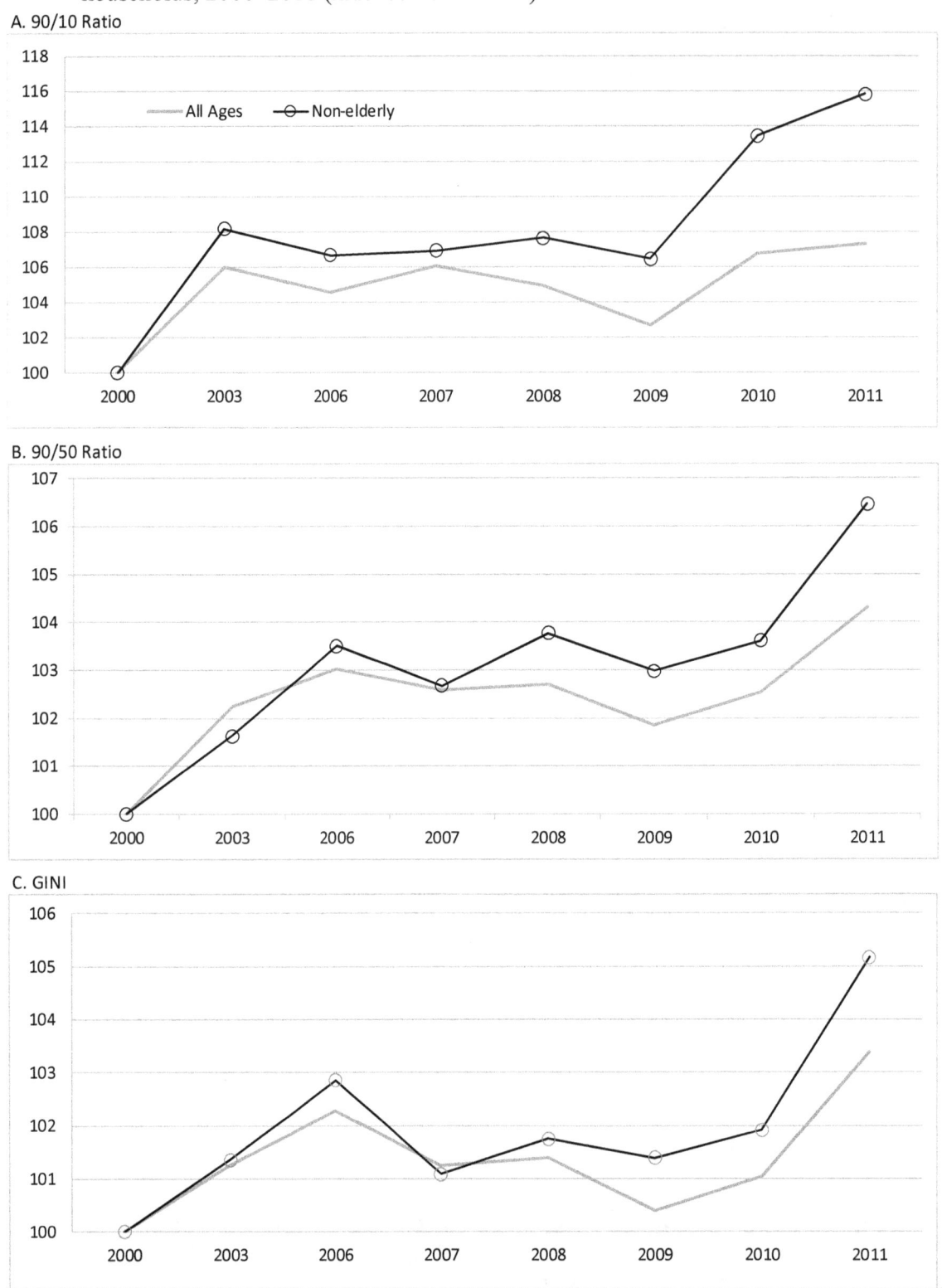

Source. Authors' analysis of March CPS (various years), CEPR extracts, and NBER Taxsim.

Figure 8. Recent Trends in Market Vs. EDHI for Non-elderly Households (2007=100)

Panel A. P90/P10 Ratio

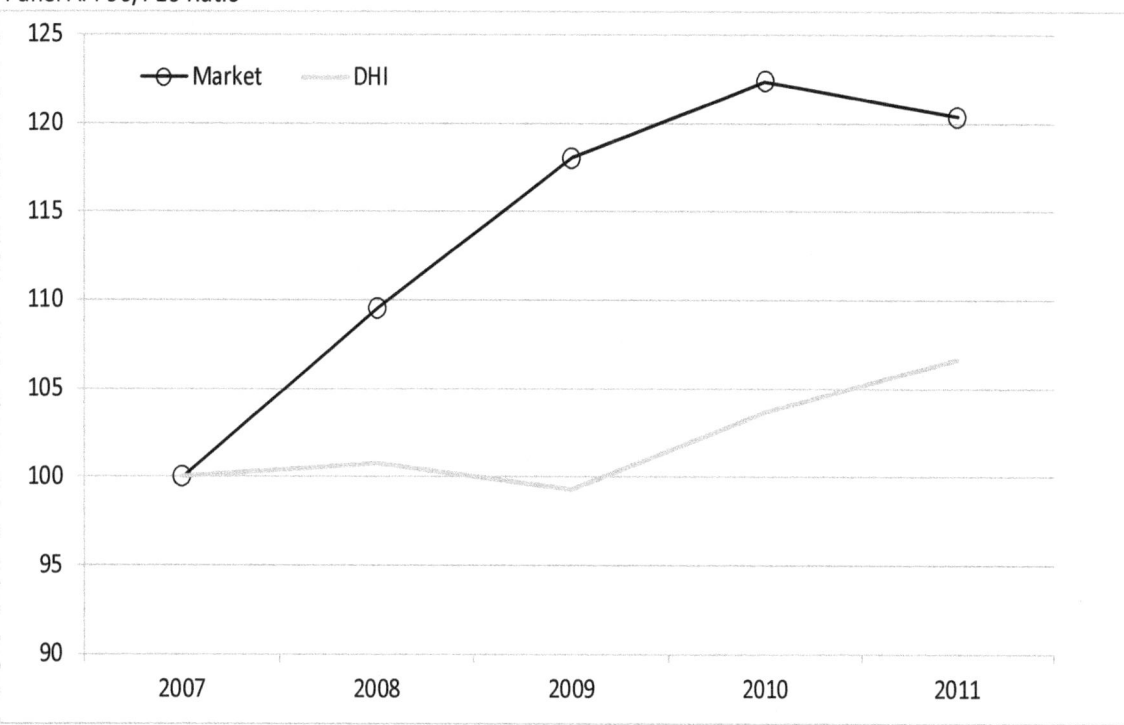

Panel B. GINI

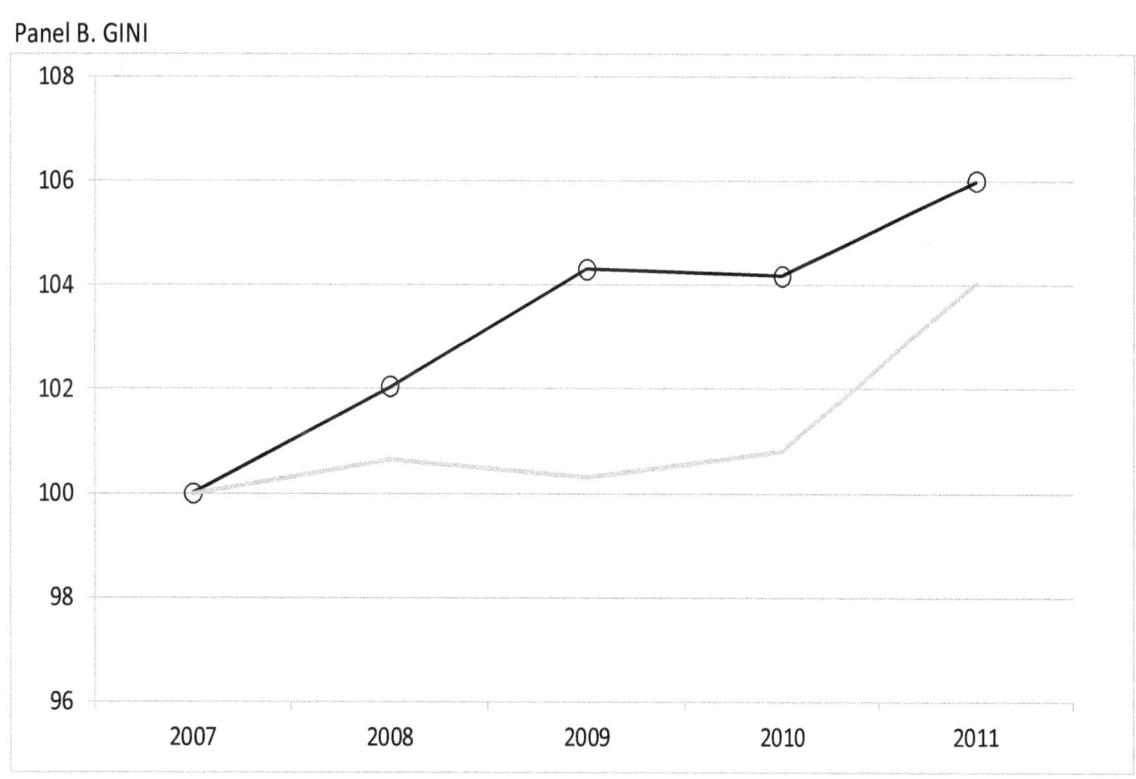

Source: Analysis of March CPS data and NBER Taxsim.

Figure 9. Top Income and Wage Shares (1960-2011)
Panel A. Top Wage Group Shares Using SSA earnings records (Mishel and Finio, 2013)

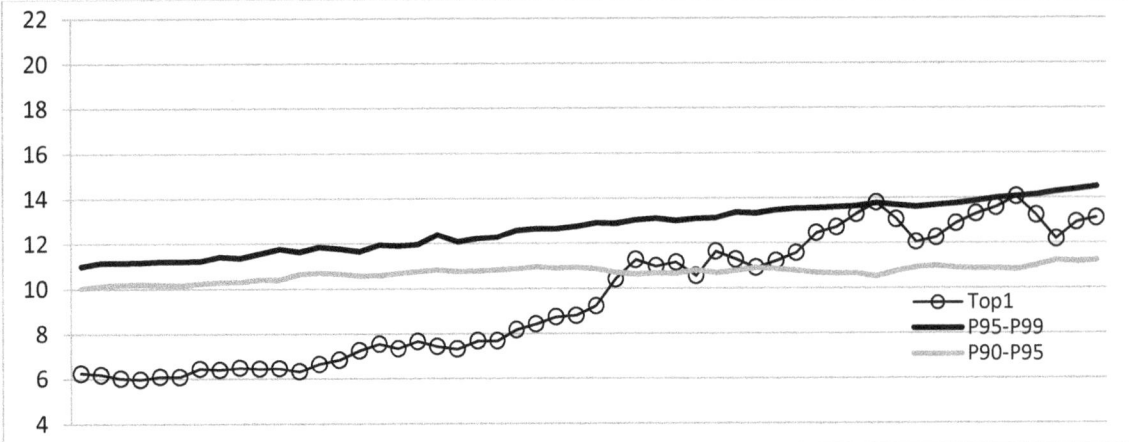

Panel B. Top Pre-tax Income Group Shares Using IRS tax statistics (PS, 2013)

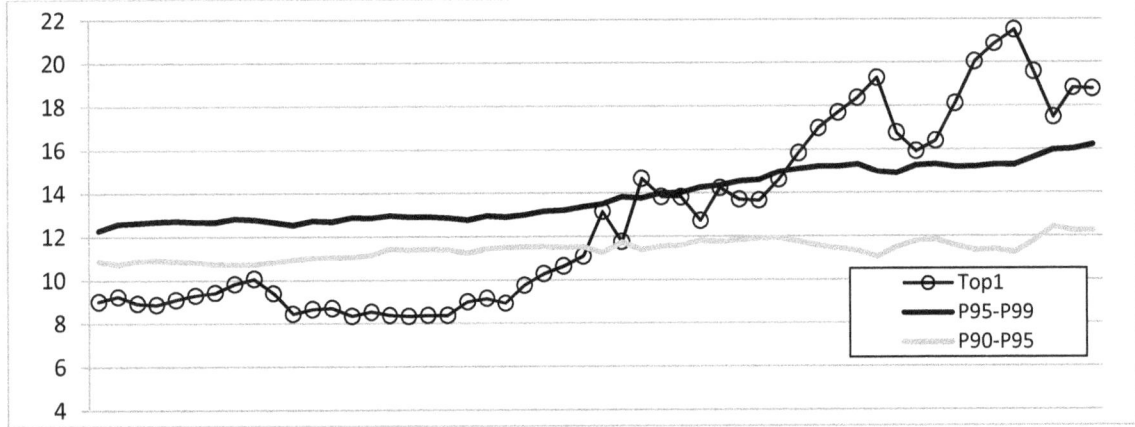

Panel C. Top After-tax and transfer Income Group Shares Using CBO "comprehensive income" (CBO, 2012)

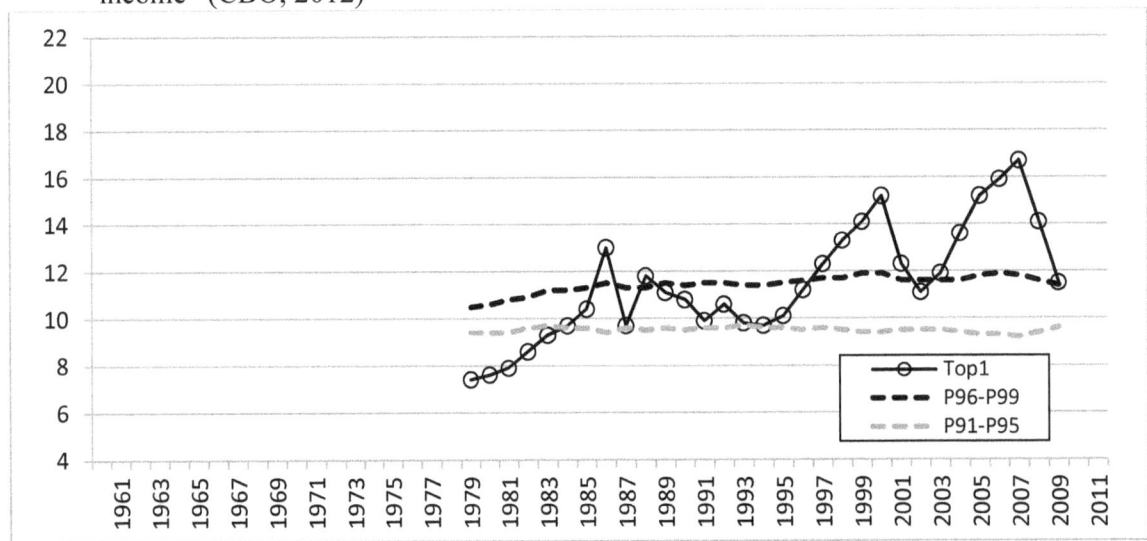

Sources: Panel A. Economic Policy Institute (2013) and Kopczuk, Saez, and Song (2010) analysis of Social Security Administration wage records. Panel B. Piketty and Saez (2013 update) analysis of IRS tax statistics. Income includes capital gains. Panel C. CBO (2012).

Figure 10. Top 10 Percent Share of Income (1960-2011) Including State-level Data

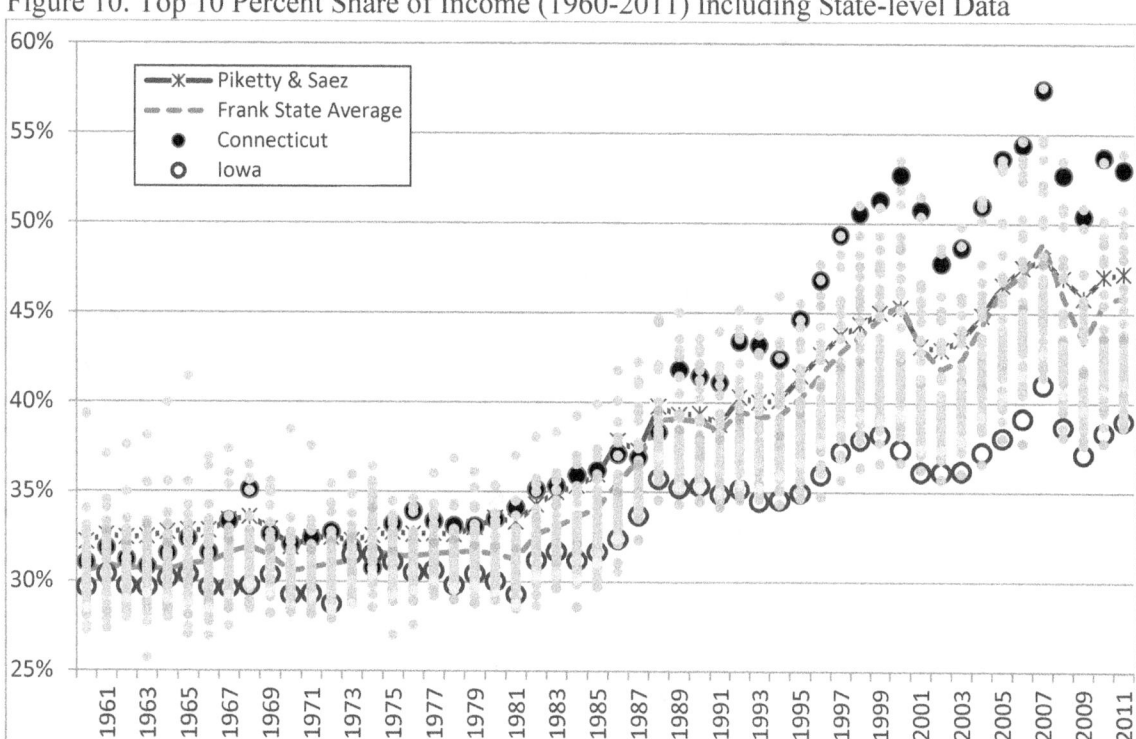

Notes: Each "dot" represents the top share for each state each year, with larger dots representing the highlighted states (CT & IA). Frank's (2009) state-level income shares are calculated for 1960 to 2005 using state-level income and tax distribution tables produced by the IRS, while Piketty & Saez calculate the national totals with the underlying IRS administrative data files. We have updated Frank's series to 2011 using more recently published state level tables, and calculated a state average that is weighted by total state personal income.

Figure 11. Income share of top one per cent, by data source, 1979–2011

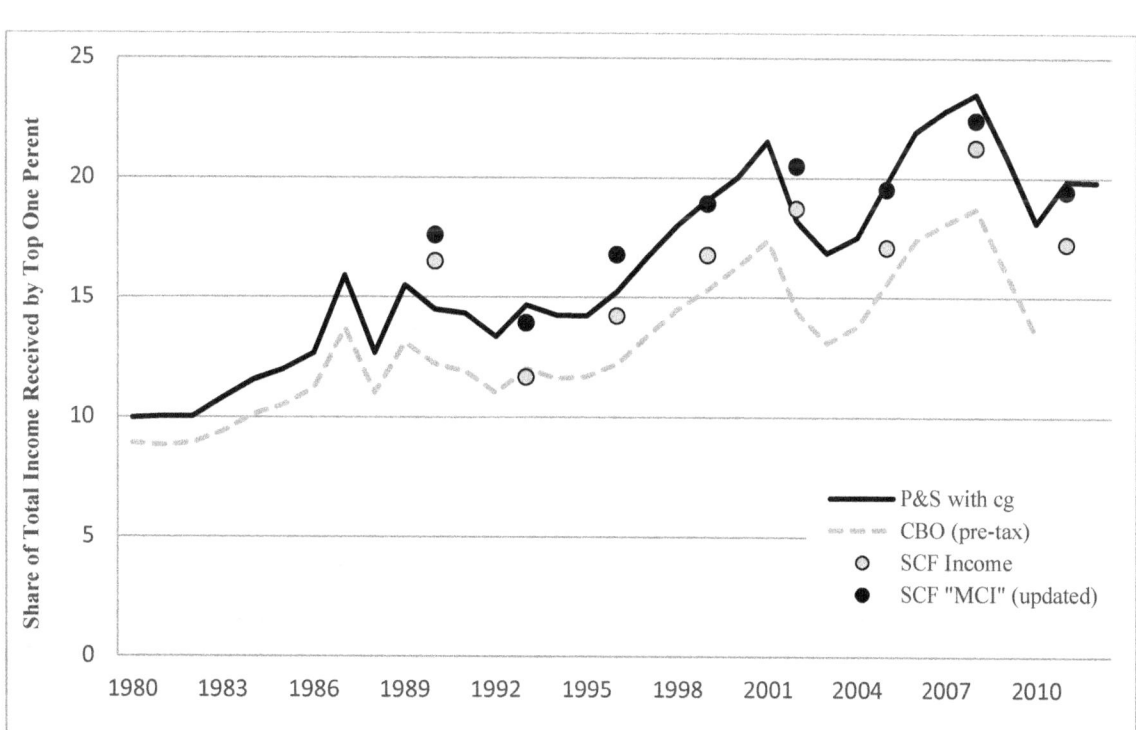

Sources: See Smeeding and Thompson (2011) (updated).

Figure 12. Household and Family poverty rates, US Official and 60% of median, Census 'money income', 1979–2011 (indexed 1979 = 100)

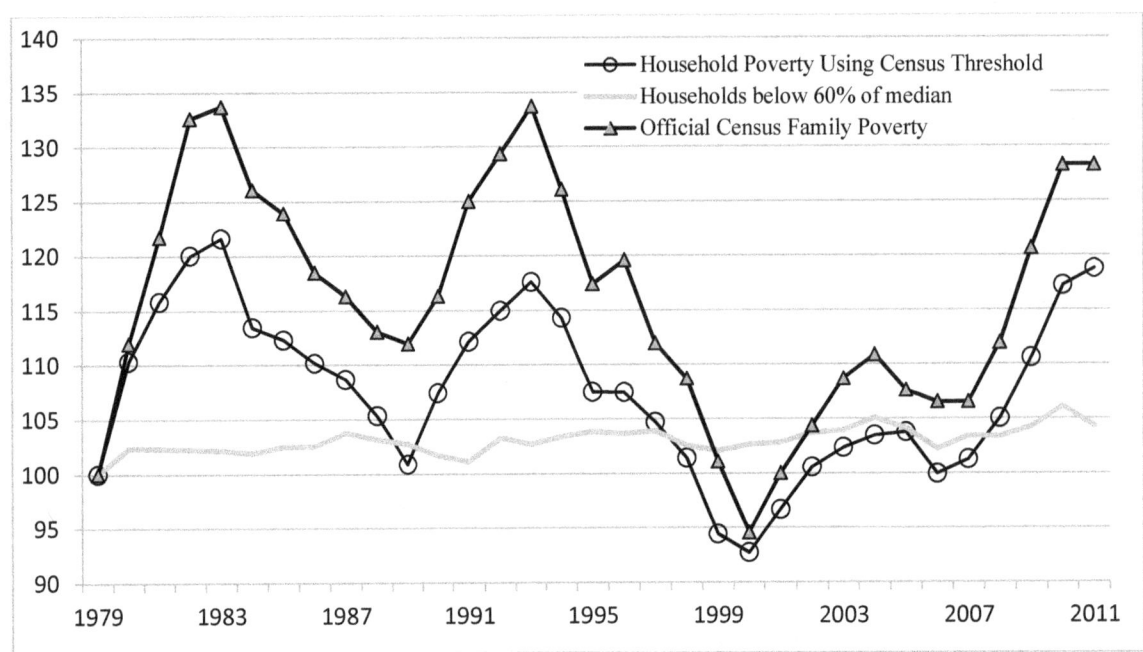

Source. Authors' analysis of March CPS (various years).

Figure 13. Household poverty rate (%), by age of household head

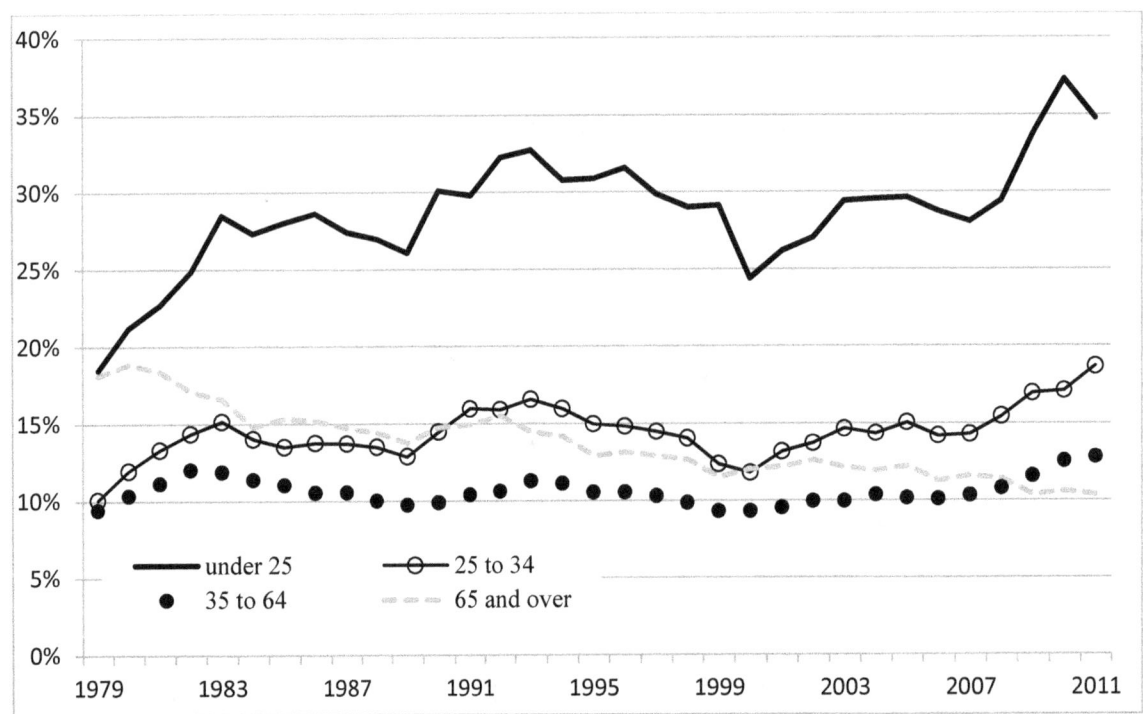

Source. Authors' analysis of March CPS (various years).

Figure 14. Household poverty rate (%), by presence of children, households with head aged less than 55

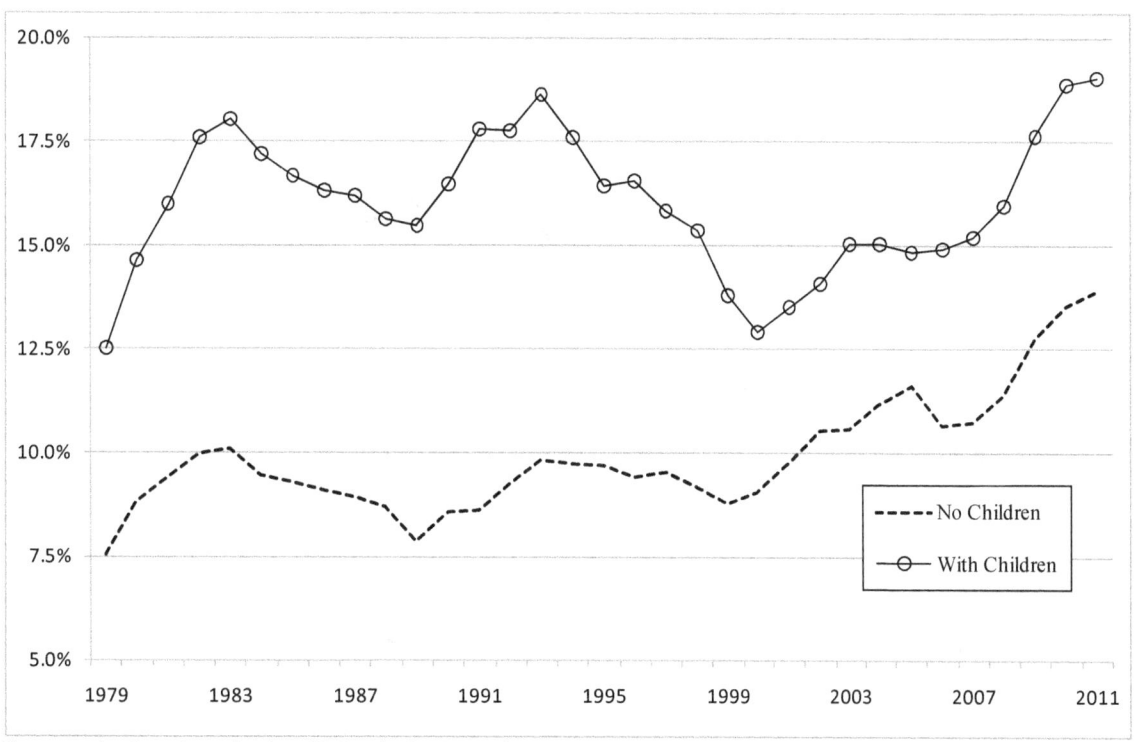

Source. Authors' analysis of March CPS (various years).

Figure 15. Post Tax/Transfer Poverty Rates (for Individuals) by Age Group (NAS definitions)

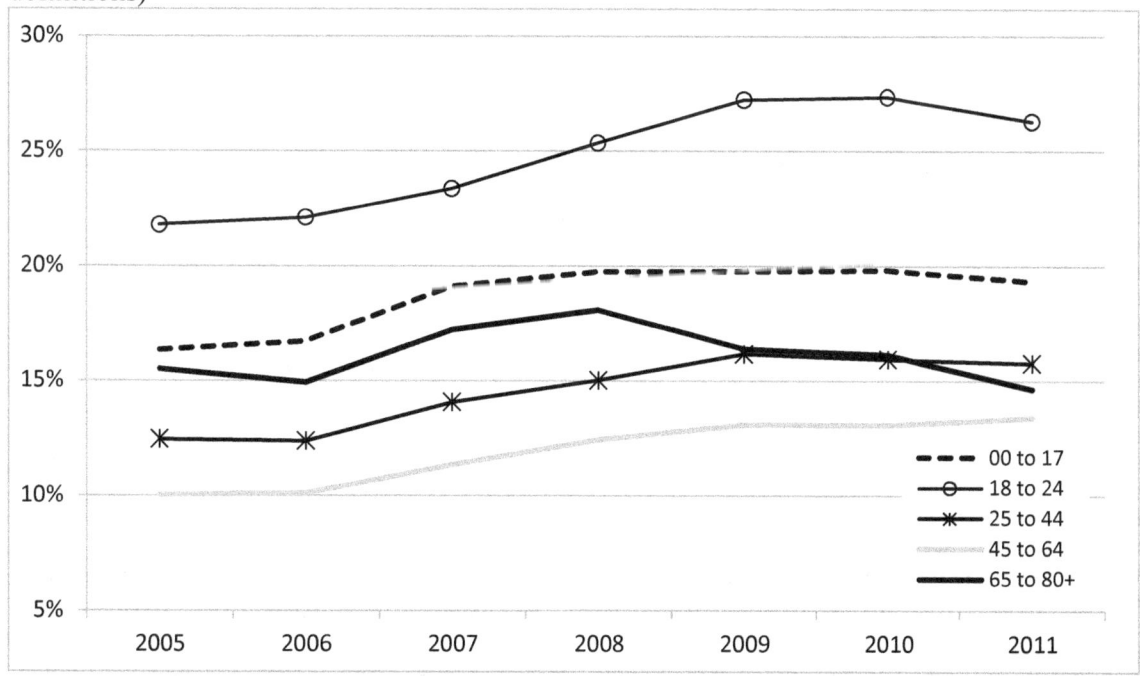

Source: Author's analysis of Census Data, retrieved from CPS Table Creator on April 30, 2013 (http://www.census.gov/cps/data/cpstablecreator.html#)

Figure 16. Poverty Trends (for Individuals) by Income Measure and Age Using Alternative Threshold (CES,GA,CE) (2007=100)

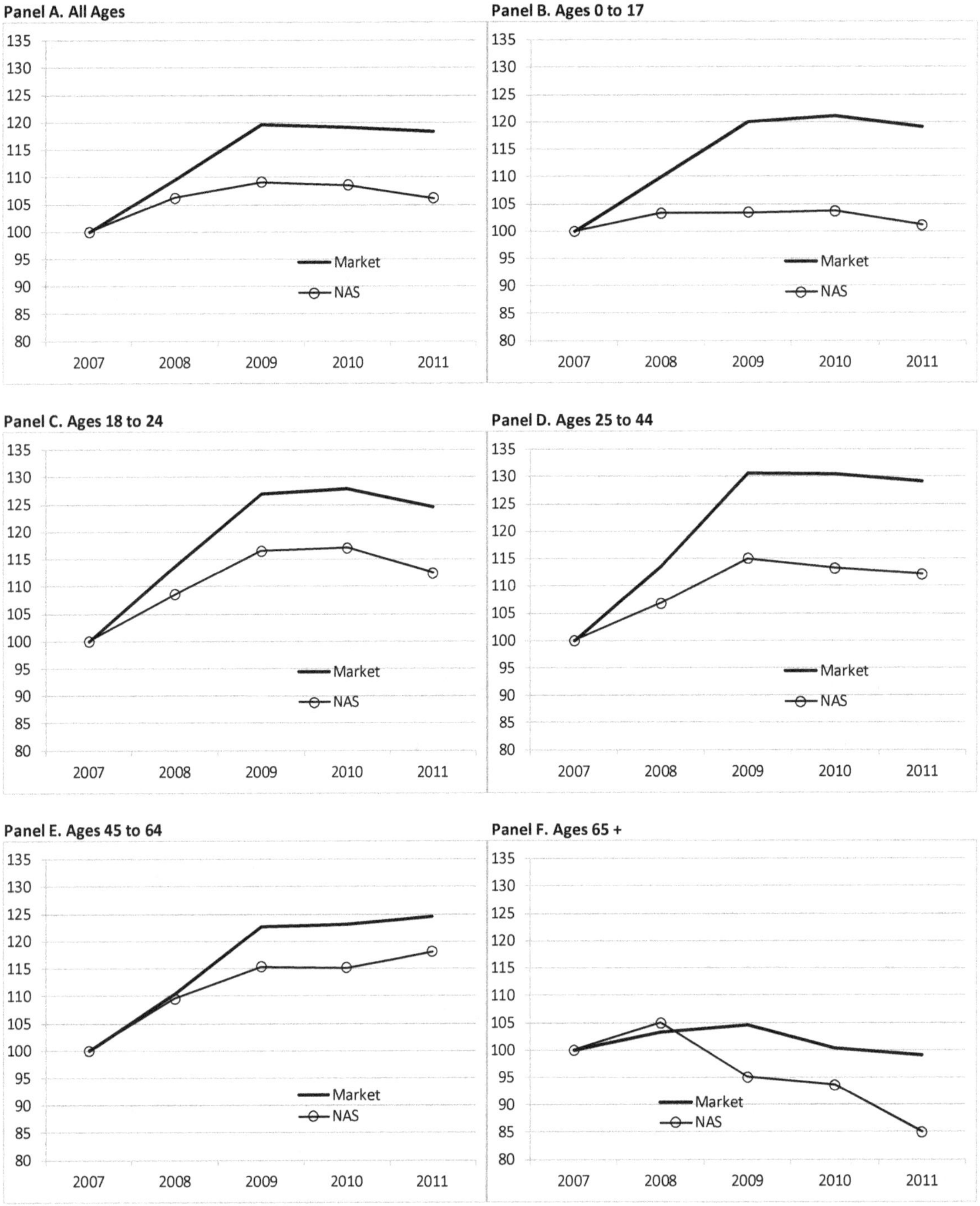

Panel A. All Ages

Panel B. Ages 0 to 17

Panel C. Ages 18 to 24

Panel D. Ages 25 to 44

Panel E. Ages 45 to 64

Panel F. Ages 65 +

Source: Author's analysis of Census Data, retrieved from CPS Table Creator on April 30, 2013 (http://www.census.gov/cps/data/cpstablecreator.html#)

Note: Market income in Figure 16 excludes imputed rent to home ownerhip. NAS income includes a broader range of transfers than "Money Income," and also excludes taxes. (See Income Definitions Appendix for more details.) Poverty thresholds in Figure 16 reflect NAS recommendations, and include cost of living adjustment based on median household expenditures, geographic cost of living adjustments, and out-of-pocket medical expenses.

Table 1. Annual real wage growth (%), by age and education group, 2007–11

	Ages 25 to 34	Ages 35 to 44	Ages 45 to 54	Ages 55 to 64
HS only				
2007 to 09	-0.3%	0.2%	1.0%	1.0%
2009 to 11	-1.5%	-2.3%	-2.1%	-1.0%
BA only				
2007 to 09	-0.1%	0.0%	0.7%	-1.6%
2009 to 11	-2.5%	-0.8%	-0.9%	-0.1%
Advanced				
2007 to 09	0.5%	1.9%	2.3%	0.9%
2009 to 11	-1.8%	-1.5%	-1.8%	-1.6%

Note. Average annual percentage change in inflation (2011$) adjusted hourly wages, adjusted for inflation using US CPI-U. Hourly wages for non-union workers.

Source. Authors' analysis of CPS ORG files, CEPR extracts.

Table 2. Comparing Equivalized Market and DHI Inequality for All Ages and Non-Elderly Households

| | Gini Coefficient | | | | | | P90/P10 Ratio | | | | | |
| | All Ages | | | Non-elderly | | | All Ages | | | Non-elderly | | |
	Market	DHI	difference	Market	DHI	difference	Market	DHI	difference	Market	DHI	difference
2007	0.464	0.374	-0.09	0.431	0.365	-0.07	14.4	5.9	-8.53	9.1	5.6	-3.47
2008	0.474	0.374	-0.10	0.439	0.367	-0.07	16.0	5.8	-10.14	9.9	5.6	-4.29
2009	0.482	0.371	-0.11	0.449	0.366	-0.08	17.4	5.7	-11.69	10.7	5.5	-5.14
2010	0.481	0.373	-0.11	0.449	0.368	-0.08	18.0	5.9	-12.10	11.1	5.8	-5.29
2011	0.489	0.382	-0.11	0.456	0.379	-0.08	17.9	5.9	-12.02	10.9	5.9	-4.95
%Change:												
2007-09	3.9%	-0.8%	-0.05	4.3%	0.3%	-0.04	20.8%	-2.9%	-0.24	18.0%	-0.7%	-0.19
2009-11	1.4%	3.0%	0.02	1.6%	3.7%	0.02	3.1%	3.8%	0.01	2.0%	7.4%	0.05

Source: Author's Analysis of CPS, using NBER TAXSIM

Note: All incomes are equivalized (divided by square root of household size)

Table 3. Shares of income components in total household income (%), by quintile group and age, 2007–11

	All Households			Non-elderly Households			Elderly Households		
	Bottom Fifth	Middle Fifth	Top Fifth	Bottom Fifth	Middle Fifth	Top Fifth	Bottom Fifth	Middle Fifth	Top Fifth
Panel A. Earnings Share									
2007	28.0%	79.7%	86.7%	43.4%	89.8%	91.1%	2.7%	27.7%	46.1%
2009	25.8%	74.0%	87.1%	37.6%	86.4%	91.5%	3.2%	22.7%	48.6%
2011	23.8%	73.1%	87.3%	34.2%	86.2%	92.1%	3.0%	22.4%	51.2%
Change:									
07 to 09	-2.2%	-5.8%	0.5%	-5.8%	-3.4%	0.4%	0.5%	-5.0%	2.6%
09 to 11	-2.0%	-0.9%	0.2%	-3.4%	-0.2%	0.6%	-0.3%	-0.3%	2.6%
Panel B. Transfer Share									
2007	66.4%	12.2%	3.2%	52.6%	6.3%	1.8%	89.0%	42.5%	15.6%
2009	68.1%	17.8%	4.1%	57.3%	10.3%	2.4%	88.8%	48.9%	18.8%
2011	70.6%	18.3%	4.1%	60.8%	10.1%	2.4%	90.2%	49.7%	17.6%
Change:									
07 to 09	1.7%	5.6%	0.9%	4.7%	4.0%	0.6%	-0.2%	6.4%	3.1%
09 to 11	2.5%	0.5%	0.1%	3.5%	-0.2%	-0.1%	1.4%	0.8%	-1.2%
Panel C. Capital (including retirement income) Share									
2007	5.6%	8.1%	10.2%	4.0%	3.9%	7.1%	8.3%	29.8%	38.3%
2009	6.1%	8.2%	8.8%	5.1%	3.3%	6.1%	8.0%	28.4%	32.6%
2011	5.6%	8.6%	8.5%	5.0%	3.6%	5.5%	6.8%	27.9%	31.2%
Change:									
07 to 09	0.5%	0.1%	-1.4%	1.1%	-0.5%	-1.0%	-0.3%	-1.4%	-5.7%
09 to 11	-0.5%	0.4%	-0.2%	-0.1%	0.3%	-0.5%	-1.2%	-0.5%	-1.4%
Panel D. Tax Share									
2007	2.2%	12.2%	24.4%	3.4%	13.6%	24.8%	0.2%	4.8%	20.8%
2009	2.0%	9.9%	23.6%	2.9%	11.5%	24.1%	0.3%	3.5%	19.7%
2011	1.6%	9.7%	23.3%	2.3%	11.3%	23.8%	0.2%	3.3%	19.8%
Change:									
07 to 09	-0.2%	-2.3%	-0.8%	-0.5%	-2.1%	-0.7%	0.0%	-1.3%	-1.0%
09 to 11	-0.4%	-0.2%	-0.3%	-0.6%	-0.2%	-0.3%	-0.1%	-0.2%	0.0%

Note. Total household income is equal to Census 'money income' plus the refundable portion of federal and state EITC and child tax credit benefits and estimated SNAP benefits. Transfer share includes estimated SNAP benefits and refundable portion of state and federal EITC and child tax credit benefits, as well as the transfer income included in Census 'money income'. Tax share excludes the state and federal EITC as well as the refundable child tax credit. Quintile groups refer to the distribution of total household income for all households.

Source. Authors' analysis of March CPS (various years), NBER TAXSIM.

Table 4. Comparing Pre- and Post-Tax/Transfer Poverty Trends (for Individuals) for Different Age Groups (Using Experimental Thresholds (CES, GA, CE))

Panel A. All Ages	2005	2006	2007	2008	2009	2010	2011	2006 to 2009 Point Change	Percent Change
A. Market Income[1]	23.9%	23.7%	25.2%	27.6%	30.1%	30.0%	29.8%	6.4%	27%
B. Market + SS, Survivors, Pensions	17.3%	17.2%	18.7%	20.8%	22.9%	22.9%	22.3%	5.7%	33%
C. NAS Income[2]	14.1%	14.1%	15.9%	16.9%	17.3%	17.2%	16.9%	3.2%	23%
D. Level Difference (C-A)	-9.9%	-9.6%	-9 3%	-10.7%	-12.8%	-12.7%	-12.9%	-3.2%	
E. Relative Difference (D/A)	-41.1%	-40.5%	-36.9%	-38.8%	-42.4%	-42.5%	-43.4%	-55.5%	
Addendum: Official Poverty Rate (Money Income and Official Thresholds)	12.5%	12.1%	12.5%	13.3%	14.2%	15.0%	14.9%	2.1%	18%
Panel B. Under 17									
A. Market Income[1]	23.7%	24.0%	26.0%	28.6%	31.2%	31.5%	30.9%	7.2%	30%
B. Market + SS, Survivors, Pensions	22.4%	22.6%	24.6%	27.0%	29.6%	29.9%	29.3%	7.0%	31%
C. NAS Income[2]	16.4%	16.7%	19.1%	19.7%	19.8%	19.8%	19.3%	3.0%	18%
D. Level Difference (C-A)	-7.3%	-7 3%	-6 9%	-8.8%	-11.4%	-11.6%	-11.6%	-4.1%	
E. Relative Difference (D/A)	-30 9%	-30.3%	-26.4%	-30.9%	-36.6%	-37.0%	-37.5%	-58.8%	
Panel C. 18 to 24									
A. Market Income[1]	25.1%	25.1%	26.3%	29.9%	33.4%	33.6%	32.8%	8.3%	33%
B. Market + SS, Survivors, Pensions	23.6%	23.8%	24.7%	28.1%	31.4%	31.6%	30.6%	7.5%	32%
C. NAS Income[2]	21.8%	22.1%	23.4%	25.4%	27.2%	27.3%	26.3%	5.1%	23%
D. Level Difference (C-A)	-3.3%	-3.0%	-2 9%	-4.6%	-6.2%	-6.3%	-6.5%	-3.2%	
E. Relative Difference (D/A)	-13.1%	-11.9%	-11.2%	-15.3%	-18.4%	-18.7%	-19.7%	-42.1%	
Panel D. 25 to 44									
A. Market Income[1]	16.7%	16.4%	17.6%	19.9%	23.0%	22.9%	22.7%	6.6%	40%
B. Market + SS, Survivors, Pensions	15.1%	14.9%	16.1%	18.3%	21.3%	21.3%	20.8%	6.4%	43%
C. NAS Income[2]	12.5%	12.4%	14.1%	15.0%	16.2%	15.9%	15.8%	3.8%	31%
D. Level Difference (C-A)	-4.3%	-4.0%	-3 5%	-4.9%	-6.8%	-7.0%	-6.9%	-2.8%	
E. Relative Difference (D/A)	-25 5%	-24.4%	-19.9%	-24.6%	-29.5%	-30.5%	-30.4%	-43.7%	
Panel E. 45 to 64									
A. Market Income[1]	16.6%	16.6%	17.9%	19.8%	22.0%	22.1%	22.3%	5.4%	32%
B. Market + SS, Survivors, Pensions	11.9%	11.8%	13.0%	14.7%	16.6%	16.8%	16.8%	4.8%	41%
C. NAS Income[2]	10.0%	10.1%	11.4%	12.4%	13.1%	13.1%	13.4%	3.0%	30%
D. Level Difference (C-A)	-6.5%	-6 5%	-6.6%	-7.4%	-8.9%	-9.0%	-8.9%	-2.4%	
E. Relative Difference (D/A)	-39.4%	-39.3%	-36.6%	-37.2%	-40.4%	-40.7%	-40.0%	-48.8%	
Panel F. 65 and Over									
A. Market Income[1]	55.7%	53.9%	55.0%	56.8%	57.4%	55.2%	54.5%	3.6%	7%
B. Market + SS, Survivors, Pensions	18.3%	17.4%	19.7%	21.0%	19.6%	19.0%	17.7%	2.2%	13%
C. NAS Income[2]	15.5%	14 9%	17.2%	18.1%	16.4%	16.1%	14.6%	1.4%	10%
D. Level Difference (C-A)	-40.2%	-38.9%	-37.8%	-38.7%	-41.1%	-39.1%	-39.8%	-2.1%	
E. Relative Difference (D/A)	-72.1%	-72.3%	-68.7%	-68.1%	-71.5%	-70.8%	-73.1%	-59.5%	

Source: Author's analysis of Census Data, retrieved from CPS Table Creator on April 30, 2013
(http://www.census.gov/cps/data/cpstablecreator.html#)

Note1: This is the Census defintion of market income less the imputed rent for home ownership. Census Market Income includes earnings (wages, salaries, and self-employment income), interest, dividends, rents, royalties, estate and trust income, non-government retirement, survivor, and disability pensions and annuities, realized capital gains (losses), non-government eduational assistance, child support, alimony, contributions, imputed return to home equity on owner-occupied housing, money income not elsewhere classified, deducting work-related expenses (excluding child care).

Note2: NAS income includes all of the components of "market" income (augmented by Social Security, Survivors and Veterans Benenfits, and Government Pensions and Annuities) PLUS unemployment compensation, worker's compensation, government disasbility pensions, public assistance (TANF), SSI, government education assistance, federal and state refundable earned income tax credits, food stamps (SNAP), free and reduced price lunches, low-income energy assistance, public housing and rental subsidies, regular price school lunches, economic stimulus payments (2009 and 2010), MINUS federal and state income taxes, payroll taxes, and childcare.

Appendix. Income definitions

Census 'money income' is defined as income received on a regular basis (exclusive of certain money receipts such as capital gains) before payments for personal income taxes, social security, union dues, Medicare deductions, and other items.

We calculated '*Equivalized Disposable Household Income (EDHI)*' by starting with 'money income' and then, 1) adding transfer income not included in 'money income' (food stamps benefits, and refundable tax credits, including the EITC and the child tax credit, 2) subtracting taxes (state and federal income taxes the employee share of social insurance (FICA) taxes (with taxes and refundable credits estimated using the NBER TAXSIM program), and 3) adjusting for differences in household size using an equivalence scale, dividing net income by the square root of household size.

CBO '*Comprehensive Household Income*' equals pretax cash income plus income from other sources. Pretax cash income is the sum of wages, salaries, self-employment income, rents, taxable and nontaxable interest, dividends, realized capital gains, cash transfer payments, and retirement benefits plus taxes paid by businesses (corporate income taxes and the employer's share of Social Security, Medicare, and federal unemployment insurance payroll taxes) and employees' contributions to 401(k) retirement plans. Other sources of income include all in-kind benefits (Medicare, Medicaid, employer-paid health insurance premiums, food stamps, school lunches and breakfasts, housing assistance, and energy assistance).

Individual Income Taxes are attributed directly to households paying those taxes. Social insurance, or payroll, taxes are attributed to households paying those taxes directly or paying them indirectly through their employers. Corporate income taxes are attributed to households according to their share of capital income. Federal excise taxes are attributed to them according to their consumption of the taxed good or service. For more information on CBO comprehensive income, see
www.cbo.gov/publications/collections/collections.cfm?collect=13

SCF Income is defined by the Federal Reserve Board as household income for previous calendar year as the following: wages, self-employment and business income, taxable and tax-exempt interest, dividends, realized capital gains, food stamps and other support programs provided by the government, pension income and withdrawals from retirement accounts, Social Security income, alimony and other support payments, and miscellaneous sources of income. See Smeeding and Thompson (2011) for more on this measure.

MCI Income: is SCF income as defined above less income from wealth (interest, dividends, rent, royalties, and income from trusts and non-taxable investments, including bonds, as well as some self-employment income) + imputed flows to stocks, bonds, annuities, and trusts + imputed flows to quasi-liquid retirement accounts (401(k), IRA, etc.) + imputed flow to primary residence + imputed flow to other residences and investment real estate, transaction accounts, CDs and whole life insurance + imputed flow to other assets and businesses + imputed flow to vehicle wealth - imputed interest flow for remaining debt (after adjusting for negative incomes). See Smeeding and Thompson (2011) for more on this measure.

NAS Income: NAS Income Consists of Census "Money Income" plus realized capital gains (losses), the federal EIC, SNAP, free and reduced-price school lunches, low-income energy assistance, public housing and rental subsidies, regular-price school lunches, economic stimulus payments (2009 ASEC only), and Economic recovery payments (2010 ASEC only). NAS income also subtracts federal income taxes after refundable credits except EIC (deducted from income), state income taxes after all refundable credits (deducted from income), payroll taxes (FICA and other mandatory deductions) (deducted from income), and work-related expenses including child care.

Table A1. Unemployment and labor force participation rates (%), 18–64 year olds

	1979	1983	1989	1992	2000	2003	2006	2007	2008	2009	2010	2011
Unemployment Rate												
Total Labor Force	5.5%	9.5%	5.1%	7.2%	3.6%	5.6%	4 2%	4 3%	5.4%	9.0%	9.3%	8.7%
By Educational Attainment:												
Less than High School	8.9%	16.6%	10.1%	14 3%	8.3%	11 2%	8.6%	8 9%	10.9%	17.2%	17.4%	16.5%
High School Only	5.4%	10.4%	5.4%	8.2%	4.4%	6.7%	5 3%	5 3%	7.0%	11.6%	12.2%	11.4%
Some College, No Degree	4.8%	8.1%	4.3%	6.3%	3.0%	5.2%	3 9%	4.0%	5.0%	8 5%	9.0%	8.4%
Bachelor's	2.9%	4.1%	2.7%	3.7%	1.9%	3.4%	2.4%	2 3%	2 9%	5.4%	5.6%	5.1%
Advanced Degree	2.0%	2.6%	1.8%	2.4%	1.3%	2.6%	1 5%	1.8%	2.0%	3.4%	3.5%	3.2%
By Age Group:												
18to24	10.7%	16 5%	10.0%	12.7%	8.0%	11.2%	9 1%	9.0%	11.4%	16.1%	17.0%	15.9%
25to35	5.1%	9.6%	5.1%	7.4%	3 5%	5.8%	4 3%	4.3%	5.6%	9.6%	9.7%	9.1%
36to45	3.5%	6.9%	3.6%	5.6%	3.0%	4.6%	3.4%	3.3%	4.4%	7.7%	8.0%	7.1%
46to54	3.2%	6.3%	3.4%	5.4%	2.4%	4.0%	3.0%	3.1%	3.9%	7.2%	7.4%	7.0%
55to64	3.0%	5.8%	3 2%	5 2%	2.4%	4 2%	2.8%	3.2%	3.6%	6.5%	7.2%	6.7%
Labor Force Participation	**1979**	**1983**	**1989**	**1992**	**2000**	**2003**	**2006**	**2007**	**2008**	**2009**	**2010**	**2011**
All 18 to 64 year olds	73.9%	75.0%	78.1%	78.4%	78.8%	77.7%	77.5%	77.5%	77.5%	76.9%	76.2%	75.6%
By Educational Attainment:												
Less than High School	63.0%	61.2%	62.5%	60.0%	62.4%	61.4%	61.6%	61.6%	60.7%	60.3%	59.4%	58.4%
High School Only	75.3%	76.1%	78.7%	78.0%	77 3%	76 1%	75.3%	75.2%	75.1%	74.2%	73.5%	72.5%
Some College, No Degree	75.6%	77.2%	80.3%	80 9%	80.8%	79 3%	78.6%	78.3%	78.3%	77.5%	76.4%	75.8%
Bachelor's	83.9%	85.7%	87.4%	87 3%	85 9%	84 9%	85.1%	84.8%	84.8%	84.9%	84.4%	83.8%
Advanced Degree	90.2%	90.0%	90 5%	91 2%	88.7%	87.3%	87.1%	87.4%	87.5%	87.2%	86.9%	87.2%
By Age Group:												
18to24	74.9%	74.0%	75 1%	73 1%	73 2%	70.3%	69.5%	68.9%	68.4%	66.7%	65.1%	64.3%
25to35	79.3%	81 5%	83 9%	84.0%	84.4%	82.7%	83.0%	83.1%	83.0%	82.5%	81.9%	81.5%
36to45	79 1%	81.7%	85 3%	85.3%	84.8%	83.9%	83.7%	84.0%	84.0%	83.9%	83.2%	82.6%
46to54	74 1%	75.7%	80 1%	81.0%	82.3%	81.7%	81.7%	81.7%	81.7%	81.2%	80.7%	80.5%
55to64	56 9%	54.7%	55.7%	56.4%	59.1%	62.5%	63.7%	63.9%	64.6%	64.9%	65.1%	64.7%

Source: authors' analysis of CPS ORG (various years), CEPR Extracts

Table A2. The distribution of real hourly wages (2011$), by education and age

	1979	1983	1989	1992	2000	2003	2006	2007	2008	2009	2010	2011
Panel A. Mean, Median and Selected PTILE Wages												
mean	17.80	17 35	17.86	17.92	19.80	20.51	20.39	20.59	20.57	21.04	20.91	20.44
p10	8.53	7.40	7.33	7.74	8.30	8.43	8.24	8.48	8 23	8.27	8.13	8.08
p50	15.04	14.80	15.10	15.20	15.80	16.47	16.49	16.03	16.21	16 53	16.26	15.76
p90	29.37	29.61	31.10	30.95	35.20	36.98	37.10	37.41	37.61	38.74	39.08	37.88
p95	35.56	37.01	38.57	38.69	44.85	46.34	47 54	48.58	48.49	49.67	49.35	48.75
Panel B. Key Inequality Measures												
P90/P50 Ratio	1.95	2.00	2.06	2.04	2.23	2.24	2.25	2.33	2 32	2.34	2.40	2.40
P90/P10 Ratio	3.44	4.00	4.24	4.00	4.24	4.38	4.50	4.41	4 57	4.69	4.81	4.69
Gini Index	0.289	0.309	0.318	0 319	0.333	0.337	0.343	0.345	0.345	0.349	0.351	0.352
Panel C. Mean Wages by Educational and Age Groups												
By Educational Attainment:												
Less than High School	14.69	13 33	12.56	11.92	11.71	12.10	11.77	11.97	11.89	12.04	11.68	11.58
High School Only	16.42	15.48	15.25	14.91	15.69	16.20	15.95	15.91	15.77	16.13	15.80	15.49
Some College, No Degree	17.56	16.81	17.09	16.91	17.92	18.30	17.91	17.99	17.73	18.01	17.75	17.23
Bachelor's	23.05	22 94	24.02	24.21	27.38	27.93	27.67	27.85	27.64	27.74	27.78	27.05
Advanced Degree	27.13	27 27	29.89	30.62	34.31	34.87	34.84	34.86	34.78	35.87	35.64	34.68
By Age Group:												
18to24	12.66	11 18	10.93	10.48	11.59	11.53	11.34	11.53	11.39	11.47	11.22	10.92
25to35	18.36	17 54	17.43	17.20	18.98	19.27	18.87	18.90	18.93	19.17	19.05	18.45
36to45	20.08	20.07	20.71	20.46	22.00	22.95	22.85	23.12	23.18	23.62	23.56	23.26
46to54	20.26	20.16	20.93	21.31	23.20	23.56	23 52	23.57	23.53	24.08	23.95	23.44
55to64	19.16	19.38	19.67	19.60	21.64	23.37	23 30	23.79	23.40	24.05	23.85	23.45

For Selected Age-Education Groups:	1979	1983	1989	1992	2000	2003	2006	2007	2008	2009	2010	2011
Ages 25 to 34												
HS only	16.66	15 50	14.92	14.41	15.09	15.48	15.03	14.86	14.69	14.79	14.59	14.33
BA only	21.30	20.89	22.26	22.35	25.13	24.93	24.35	24.27	23.98	24.22	23.92	23.01
Advanced	24.07	23.70	25.83	26.42	29.68	29.63	29.25	29.40	29.80	29.67	29.86	28.61
Ages 35 to 44												
HS only	18.00	17 18	16.67	16.23	17.22	17.63	17.36	17.44	17.15	17.51	17.07	16.70
BA only	26.58	26.42	26.50	26.56	30.12	31.26	30.77	30.97	31.09	30.98	31.09	30.49
Advanced	30.19	29.74	31.37	31.58	35.79	37.14	36.72	36.75	36.85	38.18	38.13	37.05
Ages 45 to 54												
HS only	18.37	17.86	17.54	17.26	17.49	18.11	18.07	17.88	17.84	18.22	17.79	17.46
BA only	29.10	28.40	28.27	28.60	30.40	30.59	30.99	31.12	31.34	31.54	32.21	30.96
Advanced	30.51	31.65	32.99	33.73	36.22	36.40	37.26	37.47	37.26	39.22	39.09	37.83
Ages 55 to 64												
HS only	18.29	17.60	17.01	16.77	16.96	17.75	17.43	17.54	17.30	17.87	17.58	17.52
BA only	28.01	28 94	28.69	28.33	29.25	31.36	30.31	30.88	29.81	29.87	30.35	29.78
Advanced	30.44	30 59	33.84	32.69	36.23	36.79	36.85	36.76	36.08	37.43	36.66	36.22

Source: authors' analysis of CPS ORG (various years), CEPR Extracts

Table A3. Income and Poverty

Panel A. Inflation-Adjusted Household Income

	1979	1983	1989	1992	2000	2003	2006	2007	2008	2009	2010	2011
mean	57,923	54,640	63,055	59,502	71,186	68,888	70,840	69,985	68,183	67,964	66,425	66,460
p10	12,181	11,201	12,457	11,484	13,181	12,285	12,770	12,584	12,118	12,120	11,708	11,445
p50	48,617	44,728	50,042	46,638	52,326	50,370	51,125	51,735	49,822	49,806	48,467	47,688
p90	111,332	108,238	124,490	119,272	140,060	138,421	142,382	141,189	138,300	138,000	136,772	136,864
90/10	9 14	9 66	9 99	10 39	10 63	11 27	11 15	11 22	11 41	11 39	11 68	11 96
90/50	2 29	2 42	2 49	2 56	2 68	2 75	2 78	2 73	2 78	2 77	2 82	2 87
GINI	0 399	0 409	0 427	0 429	0 456	0 457	0 462	0 455	0 458	0 459	0 461	0 469

Panel B. Inflation-Adjusted, Net, Equivalised Household Income for All Households

	1979	1983	1989	1992	2000	2003	2006	2007	2008	2009	2010	2011
mean	28,878	27,461	32,948	31,337	36,571	36,768	37,608	37,374	36,463	37,005	36,389	36,293
p10	9,846	8,995	9,947	9,530	11,337	10,944	11,298	11,229	11,038	11,352	10,849	10,754
p50	26,361	24,692	28,286	26,985	30,158	30,180	30,501	30,662	29,794	30,248	29,831	29,228
p90	49,727	48,636	58,794	56,220	65,613	67,136	68,371	68,653	66,784	67,238	66,757	66,528
90/10	5 03	5 39	5 89	5 88	5 77	6 11	6 03	6 11	6 05	5 92	6 15	6 19
90/50	1 89	1 98	2 09	2 09	2 18	2 23	2 25	2 24	2 24	2 22	2 24	2 28
GINI	0 315	0 331	0 359	0 355	0 369	0 374	0 378	0 374	0 374	0 371	0 373	0 382

Panel C. Inflation-Adjusted, Net, Equivalised Household Income for Non-Elderly Households

	1979	1983	1989	1992	2000	2003	2006	2007	2008	2009	2010	2011
mean	30,448	28,266	34,376	32,725	38,441	38,649	39,285	38,981	37,907	38,355	37,593	37,417
p10	11,110	9,139	10,475	10,017	12,401	11,703	12,085	12,076	11,712	11,877	11,053	10,825
p50	28,255	25,765	29,987	28,749	32,154	32,290	32,291	32,465	31,364	31,695	31,234	30,392
p90	50,782	49,258	60,085	57,643	67,433	68,823	70,095	70,049	68,399	68,595	68,010	68,001
90/10	4 56	5 38	5 72	5 74	5 43	5 87	5 79	5 80	5 84	5 78	6 15	6 28
90/50	1 80	1 92	2 01	2 01	2 10	2 14	2 18	2 16	2 18	2 16	2 18	2 24
GINI	0 296	0 322	0 348	0 345	0 361	0 366	0 371	0 365	0 367	0 366	0 368	0 379

Panel D. Household Poverty Measures (Using Census "Money Income")

	1979	1983	1989	1992	2000	2003	2006	2007	2008	2009	2010	2011
Household Poverty Using Census Thresholds	12 1%	14 7%	12 2%	13 9%	11 2%	12 4%	12 1%	12 2%	12 7%	13 4%	14 1%	14 3%
60% of Median	29 3%	29 9%	30 1%	30 2%	30 0%	30 4%	29 9%	30 2%	30 2%	30 5%	31 0%	30 5%
By Age of Household Head:												
Under 25	18 5%	28 5%	26 1%	32 2%	24 4%	29 4%	28 7%	28 1%	29 4%	33 7%	37 3%	34 8%
25 to 34	10 1%	15 1%	12 9%	15 9%	11 8%	14 6%	14 2%	14 3%	15 4%	16 9%	17 1%	18 7%
35 to 64	9 4%	11 9%	9 7%	10 6%	9 3%	10 0%	10 1%	10 3%	10 8%	11 6%	12 5%	12 8%
65 and over	18 1%	16 6%	13 8%	15 5%	12 0%	12 1%	11 3%	11 6%	11 4%	10 3%	10 6%	10 3%
By Household Child Status (Heads Under 55):												
No Child	7 6%	10 1%	7 9%	9 3%	9 1%	10 6%	10 7%	10 8%	11 4%	12 8%	13 6%	13 9%
Any Child	12 5%	18 0%	15 5%	17 8%	12 9%	15 1%	15 0%	15 2%	16 0%	17 6%	18 9%	19 0%
Addendum: Official Family Poverty Rate Published by Census												
Family	9 2%	12 3%	10 3%	11 9%	8 7%	10 0%	9 8%	9 8%	10 3%	11 1%	11 8%	11 8%

Source: authors' analysis of CPS ORG (various years), CEPR Extracts

Table A4. National Income and Its Disposition ($billions)

	2007	2009	2011	Changes 2007-09	2009-11
Personal income	11,912	11,867	12,947	-45	1,080
Wage and salary disbursements	6,422	6,270	6,661	-151	391
Proprietors income, rental, assets	3,291	2,896	3,252	-396	357
Transfers	1,719	2,140	2,319	422	179
Social security	576	665	713	89	49
Medicare	428	495	545	67	51
Medicaid	324	369	404	45	35
Unemployment insurance	33	131	108	99	-23
Other (Including SNAP)	286	390	441	104	51
Personal current taxes	1,489	1,145	1,398	-344	253
Disposable personal income	10,424	10,722	11,549	299	827

Source: BEA, NIPA Table 2.1, Dec. 2012 Revisions